Miracle Dogs

Miracle Dogs

Rescue Stories

Photographs and Stories by

LIZ STAVRINIDES

St. Martin's Press
New York

www.stmartins.com

Designed by Susan Walsh

Library of Congress Cataloging-in-Publication Data is available upon request.

ISBN 978-1-250-04577-5 (hardcover)
EAN 978-1-4668-4539-8 (e-book)

St. Martin's Press books may be purchased for educational, business, or promotional use. For information on bulk purchases, please contact Macmillan Corporate and Premium Sales Department at 1-800-221-7945, extension 5442, or write specialmarkets@macmillan.com.

First Edition: October 2014

10 9 8 7 6 5 4 3 2

To Debora Embody, my best friend and visionary mentor who embarked on this journey with me, and to my rescued pups who are my inspiration

A portion of the author's profits will be dontated to animal rescue and adoption efforts.

Contents

Acknowledgments

I would like to thank the following people who were instrumental in the making of this book.

Daniela Rapp—I could not have asked for a better editor. Her passion, great insights, and love for animals helped refine this book into something truly special.

The entire team at St. Martin's Press—their tireless efforts and attention to every detail was amazing!

Steve Troha at Folio Literary Management and everyone there—for seeing the vision of the book and taking it out in such a way that others saw the vision, too.

Linda Stoler—who took my idea from its infancy stage and helped strategize every step of the publishing process so my dream of this book actually became a reality.

Basia Christ—for seeing the jewels in many of the stories and helping to make them shine.

Marcy Warren, Coppy Holzman, and Laurie and Peter Marshall—for helping to bring to the book many important rescue stories that needed to be told.

Every celebrity, trainer, and rescue and assistance organization who participated in the book: No words can be put on the value you have added to this book and of course, the animals' lives you have touched.

Bill Volpi—for seeing the book's importance, his generosity, and helping to get it out to as many people as possible.

Ashley Wolf, Melisa Weiner, Teri Salpino, and Joan Perry—who helped in a variety of ways behind the scenes. They each added an important component that enriched the book in an important way.

Most especially, I want to thank all of the four-legged stars featured in this book and the wonderful families who rescued them and brought hope, love, and a whole new life to them.

Miracle Dogs

Author's Note

My heart and soul have always belonged to animals, and photography has been a passion of mine for as long as I can remember, so combining the two is only natural for me.

All of the photographs in this book were taken exclusively by me over the course of several years of meeting people and their rescued dogs. The stories of these incredible heroes and their companions were each so inspiring that I couldn't help but craft narratives to accompany the images. The result is this book. Starting with Mixer, the first dog I photographed and who now has a wonderful life with his family, to the many other pups and their forever families I've met along the way, this has been an inspiring and joyful undertaking. I've enjoyed traveling all over the country to document the lives of rescued dogs in their new, loving environments.

From the start, I have always wanted my photography to not only move people but to make a significant impact to help homeless animals. My own rescued dogs' unconditional love reminds me every day that my passion is composed in this work that I am so excited to share with you.

In the Field of Dreams

Danielle Townsend

I typically get about two kisses per year from Ashton. One on his birthday, and one on mine, maybe. Before he will agree to it, I have to wipe down my lips, and he insists on touching them to make sure they are dry. And then, the kiss is as quick as he can possibly make it. It has kind of turned into a joke in our home, but when I really stop to think about it, it's sad.

I carried Ashton in my belly for the full nine months, delivered him naturally, and had so many plans for all the hugs and kisses I would smother him with for the remainder of his life. Life didn't quite turn out like that, though. Instead, when Ashton falls and hurts himself, which is relatively often, I have to painfully watch from about two to three feet away. I wish I could grab him, kiss what hurts, and make it all better, but I now know that doing any of that will only make his pain worse. So I watch, trying to will some of his pain to transfer over to me.

When you have a child with autism, you read all these stories of how expensive treatments are, how there are a bazillion possible new causes, or how so many kids are on the spectrum now that the word *autism* has become as mainstream as *ADD* was twenty years ago. What you don't hear about as often, is the feeling of inadequacy that you feel as a parent. Suddenly, you question every decision you made during pregnancy. Are all of the therapies worth it? How much are you making the rest of your family sacrifice? I have actually had my other children say that everything we do is always for Ashton, Ashton, Ashton. And it is true. He needs more than they do. But how do you explain that to a six-year-old?

I've had feelings of guilt that we failed as parents of an autistic child. I still have not been able to reconcile with the fact that I can't comfort Ashton when he gets hurt. And even worse were the times he would disappear. I would be in the front yard pulling weeds with all the kids playing behind me. When I would look back, suddenly Ashton would be gone. No noise, no screaming, no one saw what happened to him, he would just simply disappear. Usually, it was because someone had upset him, and he decided to leave. I always found him in time before anything catastrophic happened, but I always felt that one time I might not. He has darted into elevators, right before the doors closed. He's run into the street, missed only by slow, careful drivers. I have received calls from school saying that he was missing. I was always on edge.

My feelings of incapability have always been outweighed by love, though. However tired I am, I never give up. If he needs an advocate, I am there fighting. If he needs therapy, we make it to those appointments. If there is a program that might help, I am going to make sure he is a part of it. I have no interest in curing Ashton. I think he has a lot to offer just as he is, and if I changed that, I would be doing this world a disservice. I just want to help make his way through our world a little easier. In that quest, I found Assistance Dogs of the West (ADW).

I had heard of service dogs being used as tools for people with autism a while back, and, when Ashton was almost five years old, I looked into several organizations. I chose to go with ADW because their methods were so thorough. They train rescue dogs and some dogs also come from accredited breeders. During their two years of training, the dogs live with several different people, that way they don't bond with one particular person before they are matched with their recipient. Kids help train, so the dogs get used to children giving orders, instead of just adults. People with various disabilities are also used to train the dogs. Not only does this provide jobs for these people with disabilities, but the dogs become desensitized to wheelchairs, walkers, slurred speech, or emotional outbursts. ADW has some of the most accomplished and amazing trainers and staff of any facility we visited.

We began the interview process with ADW in July 2010. They spent a lot of time getting to know us and our needs, and they listened to what I said we needed for Ashton in a dog. One of Ashton's autistic symptoms is that he has an extremely difficult time making new relationships, so he needed a dog that really wanted to bond with him. Our process took much longer than expected. We interviewed with dozens of dogs, and Ashton almost got placed with a chocolate Lab named Trevor, but Trevor developed some health problems that made our family a difficult match for him. There were times that I became a little discouraged, but ADW always assured me that we would get the right dog, and we definitely did. In June 2012 we finally found Wyatt, our little golden retriever. The first time we met Wyatt, he was only eight months old. It was love at first sight. Wyatt just knew. He knew what Ashton needed from him. He knew what I needed from

him. He knew just the right amount of energy to have. And that FACE! Really, no one can resist him.

Once we brought Wyatt home, there was an immediate change in Ashton. He began to develop a certain amount of patience and empathy that we had never seen in him before. He and his younger brother, Nathan, are now inseparable almost all the time at home. It definitely wasn't like that before. Ashton would isolate himself. Now, when I meet with school staff, they explain how Ashton is so well liked and social in class. Last spring, Ashton and Wyatt joined a Little League team for special needs kids. Ashton is a fielder and hitter, and Wyatt is the mascot and sometimes pinch runner alongside those who need to borrow him for a little encouragement. I never thought I would see Ashton play any type of sport. It's such a huge change from where we began. When we are out, Ashton loves to tell people all about Wyatt, and how he belongs to just him.

During Wyatt's training at ADW, both the trainers and Ashton worked exhaustively with hide-and-seek. Since Ashton is what we call a "bolter," we needed Wyatt to be able to find him in a hurry when Ashton disappeared. This was always one of the main goals for Wyatt. But Wyatt and Ashton had ideas of their own. Although they still love to play hide-and-seek, they have just decided that it would be better if they stayed together all the time, and that it would be better if Ashton didn't disappear anymore. It was a consequence of Wyatt being around that I had never even considered. When we are out, Ashton always holds on to Wyatt's leash, so he does not have the opportunity to wander off or hide. At home, instead of running off when he is upset, Ashton is comforted by Wyatt. Although he rejects any comfort from people, Wyatt doesn't seem to have to follow the same rules. If Ashton scrapes his knee, Wyatt comes and licks it, and then he licks Ashton's face, and then lies next to him and takes his mind off of what happened. If Ashton is having a meltdown, Wyatt comes and lies on top of him to calm him down. When Ashton needs to go to sleep, Wyatt hops in bed with him, or Ashton crawls and sleeps with Wyatt on his bed. Ashton is finally getting a good night's sleep for the first time in his life.

Has Wyatt cured Ashton? No, of course not. But Wyatt gives Ashton an outlet. He gives him protection. He gives him kisses. He gives him comfort. And by proxy, he gives the rest of us all of those things, too. I even sometimes bribe Ashton to give me a hug by telling him that I won't feed Wyatt until he does. Call it what you will, but I've easily doubled my hugs! "I'm only doing this because I really care for you!" he tells Wyatt.

I still feel like I come up short sometimes. I assume every parent does at some point. But now Wyatt is like my helping hand. Even though he has only been with us for a short time, I could not imagine life without him. He finally gave Ashton a connection to the world and for that I will always be thankful to him, and to all of those who had a role in bringing him to us.

Dingo, Foster, and Lily

What Money Can't Buy

Lance Bass

Lance Bass, who rose to fame as the bass singer for 'N Sync, has had an extended career in film and television, and most recently he was paired with the swing dance champ Lacey Schwimmer on *Dancing with the Stars*. Lance, who has a passion for music, dance, and acting, is most passionate about, you guessed it: rescue dogs!

Lance has had eight rescue dogs from animal shelters. "The nicest, sweetest loving dogs come from the pound," Lance says. "I think that they know where they come from. They started with a rough life being sent away, not being loved and wanted, and they know that, and it stays with them the rest of their lives."

"Finding a home for a dog is so fulfilling," says Lance. And who better than him to know this!

Lance is brave and softhearted, his dogs would tell you, because they know this to be true. When he went to the shelter for one dog, he came home with two, both of whom had serious injuries. They could not have survived without him. "They had suffered enough," he says.

Shannon, a friend who worked at the shelter, relayed to Lance that two dogs had just come in together. Lance was touched, and he missed having a dog since his recent move to Los Angeles.

He was stunned when the shelter manager told him of these two dogs, and their brothers and sisters, being thrown out of the window of a speeding car in a garbage bag. His heart sunk. The dogs had landed hard on the road surface. Only two had survived; these two, with major injuries.

Lance mustered his courage for what he would see as the manager led him to the crate where the dogs were housed. The dogs had been named Dingo and Foster. Lance looked at them, alive and suffering. Their injuries were multiple, terrible, and required costly care.

They had not only hit the pavement, but they had also been struck by passing cars. Dingo had two broken hips, and a torn ACL and he also suffered from cancer. Foster had two torn ACLs and a broken leg. Both dogs struggled to stand when Lance approached, and they winced in pain. Their life story had been tragic so far.

Dingo and Foster were half–Australian shepherd/half-beagle mixes. Foster was a good-sized brown-and-blond dog, and Dingo was a stockier dog with the tricolored Aussie markings of brown, black, and white.

Lance was immediately taken with them, but he felt conflicted: He had only came for one dog. His heart leaped for Dingo. Dingo was mellower and seemed resigned. Foster was more active and struggled to Lance's side, and Foster was clearly not going to let Lance go. Aussies are known to be smart dogs. Maybe Foster knew that Lance was his only chance in life, and he was going for it.

Lance relented. "It wouldn't be fair to separate them," he says. He bucked up and adopted both.

They went home, had all the surgeries they needed, fought to gain their strength, and, today, Lance says, "They are the greatest dogs ever." Dogs can have a bad start, and somehow become so filled with gratitude that love just keeps pouring from them.

Lance's heart took over again, when he fell in love with Lily. Lily was being used as bait for dogfighting. She, too, was in horrible shape when he first saw her and his heart broke. "So many dogs need a loving home," Lance says. This was the tenderness that led to fixing Lily's life. This terrier mix is playful and loving, and she is now the boss at home, along with Dingo and Foster, of course.

Dingo loves to snuggle, Foster will play catch until the cows come home, and Lily will only ride in the car on the driver's lap! Lance says, "I just love them all!"

Can't Keep a Goodman Down

Marcy Warren

Things were very hectic at our home last summer. My husband was recovering from a heart attack. I was stressed about his health. We had just lost our precious Matilda, a border collie rescue, to an illness and were still grieving. I missed her—a lot. I remember getting up one day and thinking, "I cannot handle one more crisis!"

Later that day, I received an e-mail from my good friend, Michelle Neufeld Montak, founder of the Gimme Shelter rescue organization in the Hamptons. One of her rescues, a pit bull named Katie, needed a foster home immediately. As I looked at Katie's photo, my mind flashed back to the old reruns of *The Little Rascals* series because she looked just like Petey, the gang's faithful dog.

I thought of all the strays that have physical and emotional problems resulting from abuse. Homeless. Helpless. Unloved. I remembered how hard Michelle works to find homes for them. Suddenly I quit thinking about my problems.

I called Michelle and told her that I would come to her boarding facility to meet Katie. When I arrived, she introduced me to Katie, who had no interest or connection with me at all. I was disappointed, of course. As I started to leave I saw the most beautiful white, black, and brown dog. He looked just like an Aussie shepherd/border collie, very similar to Matilda. He was so timid and shy and cowered when I went to pet him. I told Michelle, "This dog just has the greatest eyes, there is something so special about him."

Michelle began to share the details about this Aussie mix. She told me how she rescued him from Chesterfield County, a poor and very rural county in South Carolina, where people don't spay or neuter their dogs, which results in the county having a very high population of homeless animals. He was picked up as a stray by animal control one day and brought to the county kill shelter. She had no idea what his life was like before she found him at the shelter, but she said that someone must not have been very kind to him, because he would hit the ground flat if you looked his way or reached down to pet him.

"The minute I saw his face I connected with him. I saw something very soulful and vulnerable about this sweet boy, which touched me. I knew I had to save him," Michelle said. She then added: "His name is Goodman."

Halfway through Michelle's explanation, I had already made up my mind to foster him, but as soon as I heard his name, I felt it was fate.

"This must be meant to be!" I told Michelle. "My maiden name is Goodman!"

"I want to take him home to see how well he will get along with the girls," I said to Michelle. Panda and Foxy, my little Pomeranians can be very possessive and territorial.

"If you have any problems, please call right away and I'll come get him," Michelle said.

As I opened the back hatch door of my SUV, Goodman just sat there and looked at me and then looked over at the passenger door. I understood what he wanted. When I opened the front door, he jumped into the "shotgun" position. As I drove, he kept his nose out the window as if he was taking his first smell of freedom. I had tears in my eyes as Goodman's head turned to take in every sight, smell, and noise on the ride home, every once in a while licking my hand on the steering wheel.

I called and asked my husband to bring Panda and Foxy outside for their first meeting because Goodman was so skittish. When we arrived, my husband was outside with the girls. Before Goodman's paws hit the ground, Panda and Foxy welcomed him with lots of doggy kisses and they all rolled in the grass. The three dogs fell in love instantly. As the girls ran to the front door, Goodman looked at me with his expressive eyes. They seemed to say, "Thank you," as he took off to follow them.

Once in, Goodman suddenly stopped. The sound of his nails clicking on the wood flooring frightened him. He picked up one paw, but didn't put it down. He whined until my husband picked him up and put him on the carpeting.

Panda and Foxy ran past Goodman, and up the stairs they went. He ran after them, but stopped at the foot of the stairs and refused to climb. He looked at me as if he was beaten and began to cower again.

When I climbed the stairs and called for him, Goodman howled, the mournful cry of an animal in pain.

It suddenly dawned on me that Goodman had never been inside a house before.

My husband and I weren't sure what to do. We'd never had a dog that didn't know what being an indoor dog meant. In fact, Goodman was so nervous about being in the house that when my husband left for work the next day, and every day for a week afterward, Goodman bolted out of the door behind him and ran down the street howling in the opposite direction. I became known in our neighborhood as "the crazy lady in the robe chasing a dog down the street yelling, 'Goodman, come back!'"

It took weeks and lots of love to get Goodman to trust my husband and me. We literally had to take the smallest steps to get him used to walking on the wood floors and climbing the stairs. Once this was accomplished, we still had the challenge of getting Goodman to come down the stairs. I think someone must have thrown or kicked him down the stairs because he would howl and curl up in a ball if we stood behind him.

With each day that passed, we gained a little more of Goodman's trust. We have such a deep bond, I can almost read his mind. I know when he's frightened or happy or curious. Today, Goodman has free run of the house. He is definitely the pack leader of Panda and Foxy.

I was initially drawn to Goodman because of his amazing eyes. I saw something special in them and my intuition proved to be right. He is loving and kind, and the best boy ever. There is something so special about dogs that have been rescued. They are loyal and respond quickly to love. In Goodman's case, his eyes say it all: "Thank you for giving me a loving home." And I thank Goodman every day for coming into our lives.

4   Jake, Trooper, and Sage

From Trauma to Trust

Andrea Eastman

What does a casting director and agent, well-known in Los Angeles and New York City, who has it all, do after living in the fast lane?

One woman who fits that description is seventy-two-year-old Andrea Eastman. She left her glamorous life behind and purchased a twenty-plus-acre ranch in Montana. This tiny woman, with a large capacity of love, vowed to help creatures who cannot help themselves—abused animals.

She has three rescue dogs—Jake, Trooper, and Sage—as well as four rescue horses—Shawnee, Lucky, Indiana, and Chevy. This amazing woman has no volunteers and does the bulk of the work herself—heavy, never-ending work. Every day is a very full day of feeding, grooming, training, caring for, and loving each animal.

Jake, a handsome black-and-white border collie, was approximately ten months old when animal control officers found him on the streets of Los Angeles. He was severely malnourished and traumatized from the horrific abuse he suffered as a puppy. He was adopted by a young mother and her son, who returned him because of his unearthly howl. Andrea described it as coming from the depths of the hell his soul had sustained. "There must have been so much this poor dog experienced in his early years that caused him to release the pain through his wailing, which shook me to the bone," she said.

After Andrea adopted him, however, it took another nine months before he was able to let go of the agony of the terror he experienced and let her get close to him. Several years later, Andrea finally was able to convince Jake that he was in a safe place and that she would not harm him. Even after thirteen years in her loving care, Jake will snap at anyone who tries to approach him when he's lying down, except Andrea, of course.

Andrea said, "Jake has come a long way, yet his eyes look right through you, still showing the pain inflicted upon him." If you look closer, you can also see the depth of the wisdom he has gained from this caring woman.

When Jake was approximately seven years old, Andrea hoped he was ready for her to bring another rescue dog home. This time it was a handsome and sweet blond retriever. The dog was locked in a too-small crate for twelve hours on a plane, and never made a mess, as he flew to his forever home with Andrea in Montana.

When Andrea picked him up at the terminal, she said, "I took one look at the dog and named him Trooper, because he was and is. I was a bit concerned about how Jake would react to our newest family member. As soon as Trooper and Jake met, instead of the normal sniffing, Trooper wrapped his paws around Jake's neck and held on for dear life . . . and Jake let him." And this is how they greet each other to this day.

While Jake took quite some time to be house-trained, Trooper learned in three days. Andrea believes it is because Jake showed Trooper the ropes.

Wherever Andrea goes, Trooper is close. She is never out of his sight, unless you're a guest in her home. Then you might catch him sneaking into your suitcase and carrying off a bra, underwear, or whatever he grabs first, to show Andrea. Trooper also follows closely behind when Andrea takes one of her horses for a ride. He is her protector because they share the greatest gift a human and dog can have, a bond based on unconditional love and trust.

Because of the success Andrea had with the two dogs, she felt confident another dog could be added to her growing pack.

Sage, a beautiful, sienna-colored retriever, was picked up by animal control officers after a neighbor reported her owner for severe neglect and abuse. The dog was taken to the pound, and, although she is a gorgeous dog, she was not being adopted because people could not get close to her. If anyone came near her, she would cower in fear and shake; reactions from being beaten so many times. When Andrea saw her, she looked beyond the dog's behavior and, instead, looked into Sage's soul and saw more than a dog whose spirit was beaten; she observed a longing for someone to love and care for her.

"In the beginning, Sage had to be coaxed to eat," Andrea remembered. To this day, she doesn't know why. Sage might have been around other dogs that fought her for food or perhaps she was poisoned. Andrea tried every brand of dog food and cooked elaborate meals of healthy meat and vegetables. "I don't think it was the quality of the food. I think it was a matter of me gaining Sage's trust. After two years, Sage now looks forward to mealtimes and even celebrates by doing a dance as I get her bowl ready," Andrea said.

When company comes, Sage is the first one to the door to welcome the guests. She greets them by sharing one of her favorite squeaky toys, then gently takes their hands and leads them to the guest room. She will give up her bed in the kitchen and sleep on the floor of the guest's bedroom, making rounds during the night to make sure everyone is safe.

Andrea adopted dogs most people wouldn't—dogs that needed a lot of time to feel safe, dogs that showed signs of aggression after experiencing abuse at the hands of their owners, and dogs that, when given loving care and a safe environment, become wonderful companions.

Andrea has learned that our lives will not be measured by how much we make, how successful we are, how famous we are, or how many cars, houses, diamonds, or boats we own. We will not be judged by what we do when someone is watching, but by what we do when no one is. Each of us, when we are standing in judgment, will have our lives measured by how well or badly we treated our fellow human beings and God's creatures.

The Gentle Barn

Ellie Laks

The Gentle Barn was founded by Ellie Laks in 1999, and it is now run by Ellie and her husband, Jay Weiner, who joined forces in 2002. The Gentle Barn is currently home to 130 animals who were rescued from severe abuse, neglect, or slaughter. Once the animals are rehabilitated, they stay at the barn for the rest of their lives and serve as ambassadors, helping to heal abused children. The Gentle Barn is host to kids in foster care, on probation, in gangs, on drugs, or from the inner city, as well as school groups and special needs kids and adults. Through the interactions with the animals and their stories, kids learn kindness, compassion, confidence, and reverence for all life.

The Gentle Barn had been a dream of Ellie Laks's since she was seven years old. She would bring homeless or injured animals home and her parents would get rid of them while she was in school. When she came home to find them gone, Ellie would say that when she grew up she would have a huge place full of animals, and she would show the world how beautiful they are.

Ellie and Jay had similar childhoods where they both felt alone, unseen, and misunderstood. Both of them received their attention, friendship, and unconditional love from animals. Having been saved by animals, it was their dream to have a place that allows children to be supported and healed by animals like they had been. Ellie and Jay see their 130 rescued farm animals as teachers, healers, friends, and heroes. Every animal at The Gentle Barn has been rescued from horrible abuse, neglect, and loneliness, and yet they have all survived by being forgiving, trusting, loving, and courageous. These are the qualities that Ellie and Jay strive for on a daily basis, and what they teach the children who visit The Gentle Barn.

Ellie and Jay live on the property with their three children and their own rescue dogs. The following are the rescue stories of their dogs.

Kaylee's Story

Kaylee was hit by a car in a bad neighborhood. We scraped her off the street and took her to the hospital. Little did we know that healing her body was only the first step. Once her body was better, our real work had begun. When we brought her in the house or car, she would start convulsing and throwing up in fear. It took us a year and a half to reassure her that she was safe and welcomed in the house as part of our family. She is the only dog we know of who survived Cushings, a disease that affects the function of many organs in the body.

Now she is a therapy dog to the kids who come here to be healed.

Socks's Story

Socks was adopted and returned three times to the animal shelter. She is completely nocturnal, can jump over any fence, and has more energy than one household can accommodate. She was hours away from euthanasia when we brought her home to The Gentle Barn. Here she can be herself, and she will have a home with us forever.

Maddie's Story

Maddie was homeless for the first several years of her life. She trusted no one and ate out of garbage cans to survive. At one point she was hit by a car, which slowed her down enough that she could finally be caught.

Once her body was healed, we worked tirelessly to teach her to trust us. It took years, but she is finally a normal and happy member

of our family who greets people at the door with tail wags, and even sleeps in bed with us.

Rover's Story

Rover was minutes away from being put down at the shelter when we found her. Shaking at the back of the cage, she would not let anyone get close to her.

Once safe at our home, it still took her many years before she did not convulse at the sight of a person. Rover has finally put the past behind her and not only crawls into our laps, but demands our attention. She has made a full recovery here.

Dylan's Story

Dylan's person died suddenly and Dylan was locked in the house for a week with no food, water, or way out. Finally someone discovered him, and he was taken to the animal shelter. Dylan was adopted,

but had horrible separation anxiety, so he was brought to the Gentle Barn to heal. So far he is doing well here. He is very happy and already part of the family!

Bingo's Story

Bingo was abandoned in someone's yard when he was only six weeks old. The family that found him was going to keep him, but they were in the military, and were transferred out of state. He was so young, had already gone through two abandonments, and had separation anxiety. We couldn't bear to hurt him again, so we kept him. He can now trust our love and knows that he will never be left again.

My New BFF

Hoda Kotb

Kathie Lee Gifford gushed about her love for her dog, Bambino, an adorable little white Maltipoo, to her cohost on the *Today* show, Hoda Kotb. Kathie Lee brings Bambino regularly to the studio, and he wags and wiggles on camera, showing the viewing audience how much love they share. Hoda had been wanting a dog for a long time and after seeing the connection between Kathie Lee and Bambino, Hoda took a leap, and worked with the rescue group PAWS Chicago and Petfinder to find her new love. Her story and search for her new best friend was documented live on the *Today* show, and created a great deal of buzz for how the two were transformed by finding each other.

After she announced that she was going to adopt a dog, the show scheduled a great event of ten tail-wagging pups in New York City's Central Park. The pups were all there to grab Hoda's heart; she took three of them home with her for a "master date."

Hoda could not help but fall for the five-month-old black and white cockapoo. "He was not a dog that I thought that I would select," said Hoda. "But when you know, you know!"

"I love this dog, Kath," she gushed to Kathie Lee on air. "He's the absolute best dog ever!"

Kathie Lee replied, "If you are lucky, he'll be with you for a long, long time and will be the best friend you ever had!"

Cinnamon, an eight-week-old poodle mix also found a new home on the show. Kathie Lee adopted Cinnamon for her friend Taryn and her son.

PAWS Chicago, the nonprofit pet rescue organization, had rescued Hoda's new love from the city pound after he was found as a skinny, mangy, flee-bitten stray wandering hopelessly on a side street of the city. Sadly, thousands of homeless pets are euthanized in Chicago each year. Paula Fasseas, PAWS founder, is thrilled that Hoda spotlighted her organization, saying, "When notable people adopt and draw attention to the tragic reality that so many wonderful homeless animals are killed every year, it brings the importance of adoption to the public's attention and saves thousands of lives. Since the show aired, the phones at PAWS have been ringing nonstop with people wanting to adopt."

PAWS Chicago's "no kill" mission and lifesaving programs have attracted other notable adopters including Billy Corgan, the frontman for Smashing Pumpkins, and Oprah Winfrey, who adopted her last three dogs—Sadie, Sunny, and Lauren—from PAWS.

How did the adorable cockapoo get his name? Hoda admits that she is star-struck with the famous country singer Blake Shelton, but she didn't think she would have the nerve to name her dog after him. She picked the name Charlie to be safe. However, after hearing of her dilemma, Blake called in on her show and said that he would be personally hurt if she *didn't* name the dog after him. So Hoda announced on the *Today* show that Blake Charlie was the object of her love and affection.

This rescue puppy is looking forward to a transformed life, new hope, and a bright tomorrow thanks to his new mom, pet-parent Hoda.

As Hoda said, "This has been a life-changing event for me!"

7   Goobers

The Dog in the Gilded Cage

Jennifer Miller

Dogs can be rescued from places other than shelters or kill centers. Sometimes they come from a world where they are pampered, receive the best of everything, and are part of what the American Kennel Club calls "a great sport where the thrill of competition is combined with the joy of seeing beautiful dogs."

Yes, these dogs have a life many of us might envy. They are show dogs, the best of their breeds, perfect specimens that are bred to continue an auspicious lineage. They are worth thousands of dollars, and their puppies are sold to people who are willing to spend big bucks for their bloodline. Their owners spend thousands more on training and care.

However, these animals are treated as commodities, not members of a family. They are not petted; they are groomed. They aren't allowed in the beds of their owners; they live in shipping crates on the road going from show to show. They aren't held with love; they are poked and prodded by unemotional judges. They don't play with their owners; they are meticulously trained by handlers who keep them for months at a time.

This is the world in which a chocolate-colored cocker spaniel named Buster Brown lived. He was a champion. His owner planned on breeding him so he was never neutered. Buster knew how to strut his stuff. He knew how to respond to the judges and play to the crowds. He knew what was expected of him.

When the owner lost interest in doing dog shows and breeding him, she gave Buster Brown to a woman who runs a cocker spaniel rescue out of her home. His name was changed to Cheyenne, but the dog had not been socialized to live in the "real" world. Because he wasn't neutered, he was kept in a crate and only taken out a few hours daily for a year and a half. During this time, his new owner had been trying to find a home for him.

My friend Rebecca heard about the situation and said she had a friend, who was looking for a cocker spaniel and would like to meet him.

The woman was ecstatic. She knew Cheyenne deserved to have a home where he would be loved. When I came to meet Cheyenne, the woman was surprised when the dog responded to me so quickly.

The woman told me that "when others have come to meet him, he has been standoffish." With me, he acted like a puppy, probably for the first time in his life. I took one look at this chocolate fur ball and said, "I'm going to change his name to Goobers because he looks like a chocolate-covered peanut. And because he's so sweet."

Goobers and I bonded on the drive home. He lay close to me on the front seat. As I petted his thick fur, he turned his head and licked my hand. I figured we would have no problems once we got home. After all, he was the most obedient, well-trained dog I had ever been around.

I've had dogs before, but nothing prepared me for teaching a dog to be, well, a regular dog.

It was quite a change from the life he had. Goobers took a while to get used to having the run of our apartment. When my husband, Mark, threw a ball for Goobers to fetch, he just looked at it. He didn't know what to do. He hadn't ever played with toys. On the other side of the coin, when we went for a walk, he strutted through the park as if he owned it. People commented on how beautiful he was and how well he behaved.

It's so heartwarming now to see how excited he gets when he is surprised with a new toy. He throws it up in the air, then runs around and around, playing for hours until he conks out using his new treasure as his pillow.

Many of my clients, and some famous ones, too, like Hoda Kotb, Barbara Walters, and Mila Kunis, visit my stores just to admire Goobers.

He still is groomed, pampered, and photographed, though now for fashion and home magazines. He is somewhat of a rock star with a huge fan club. Goobers goes everywhere with Mark and me. Every Christmas Eve, we all travel to our favorite getaway in Zihuatanejo, Mexico.

Goobers has gone from being just another beautiful dog on the dog circuit who was judged in an arena before a crowd of strangers, to an important part of our family. He became the child we never had.

8 Marvin

The Mighty Wonder Dog

Bill Volpi

My dad, Chuck, and my mom, Bernice, are in their eighties and my mom is legally blind. For years, their longtime companion was a black Lab named Abby. After Abby passed away from cancer, they both mentioned how empty their home felt. When I visited, I could also see the emptiness in their eyes as if they had lost their best friend.

A few months later, I asked if they were ready to bring some life back into their home. They looked at each other as if they had won the Mega Millions jackpot. They didn't even have to answer. The search for their new best friend began that day.

Just as they had rescued Abby from a local pound, my parents wanted to do the same for another dog. I drove them to the local ASPCA facility with high hopes of finding the right dog for them. My parents wanted a mature dog and one who was house-trained and friendly.

As the attendant walked us slowly down the rows of cages, every dog ran to the front, barking or whining or trying to lick our hands. As we approached the end of the last row, I saw one dog who did not act like any of the others. This dog stood with its face pointed toward the wall. I couldn't get a clear look at its face and bent down to see if I could get a better view. I quietly said, "Hello," and the dog turned around quickly, unafraid. He ran to where I was kneeling and licked my hand as I put it inside the cage. The look from his eyes traveled right to my heart and I knew he was the one.

The attendant explained Marvin was about a year old and was part pit bull and, therefore, potential owners were normally interviewed to ensure they weren't going to use the dog for fighting. The attendant smiled as he looked at my parents and knew their intention was to love the dog and give it a good home, so the decision was made to waive the strict interviewing process and let us take him home that day.

My parents were thrilled as Marvin took his seat in the back with my dad as we drove home as if he had done it before. Since that moment, the bond between the two of them has only gotten stronger. My dad always took Marvin out for a morning drive and afterward, my mom prepared and joined them on the porch for breakfast.

Marvin's temperament is perfect for an elderly couple. He always sat patiently as my mom carefully prepared his favorite meals. Marvin calmly waited for my dad to sit before taking his place next to my dad's chair on a specially made blanket.

Although my parents weren't able to walk Marvin, he didn't seem to mind. He followed them around the house and sat when they did. He loved when my mom gently rubbed his back; he loved when my dad roughhoused with him and threw the stick in their yard for a rousing game of fetch.

One summer afternoon, my dad was doing some repairs on the driveway. Marvin was at his side as usual. As he bent down to pick up a tool, my dad slipped on the gravel and hit his head. He tried hard to get up, but just didn't have the strength. Marvin ran back and forth as if to encourage my dad to get up.

When that tactic didn't work, Marvin ran quickly into the house and barked frantically, which was not normal. My mom knew something was wrong because my Dad was not with Marvin.

When she looked outside the kitchen window and saw my dad, hurt and bleeding on the ground, she instantly called 911. By the time the ambulance arrived, Marvin was again by my dad's side, licking the blood from his face and head. Marvin sat quietly next to my dad as the paramedics took his vitals. When it was determined Dad needed more help, Mom and Marvin rode in the ambulance to the hospital, where I met them.

A few months later, my mom felt ill and got up during the middle of the night to get the medicine she kept in the kitchen. It was dark and, because she has a hard time seeing anyway, she lost her footing and fell in the hallway before she made it to the kitchen. She was disoriented and frightened. Her first call for help went unanswered.

With her second cry, Marvin awakened instantly. He ran to her and somehow knew what must be done. He quickly turned around, and charged back into my parents' bedroom, barking and jumping up on the bed, which he was never allowed to do. He woke my dad from a sound sleep and wouldn't stop barking until my dad got out of bed. At first my dad scolded him for waking him up, but when Marvin wouldn't stop barking, my dad realized my mom wasn't in bed. Marvin then led my dad to where my mom had fallen.

As my dad gently helped my mom to her feet, Marvin stood behind them, waiting quietly to see if any other assistance was needed. My dad called 911 and the paramedics, who were the same team that had treated my dad earlier that summer, were surprised to learn Marvin had alerted my dad as he had alerted my mom.

One of them assessed my mom's injuries, while the other determined that they could treat her safely at home. As they finished treating my mom's injuries, one mentioned what a wonderful dog my parents had and the other interjected how lucky Marvin was that they rescued him. My dad smiled and countered with, "No, we're the lucky ones. We probably wouldn't still be alive if it wasn't for Marvin."

A few years have passed and my mom has Alzheimer's, and she now resides in a rest home in King of Prussia, Pennsylvania, not far from our family home where my dad and Marvin still live together. My dad uses a walker today, and Marvin is still never far from his side to make sure he doesn't fall. I travel from Brooklyn, New York, each weekend so that we can all visit Mom. Marvin is a big hit with the residents, the nurses, the doctors, and other staff.

Marvin not only brought life back into my parents' home, he also saved their lives and continues to bring life into the rest home. He truly is Marvin, the wonder dog!

Miss Molly

Pia's Passion

Pia Grønning

Rescuing animals is not a new phenomenon; however, more and more people are becoming advocates for God's creatures that have no voice of their own.

One woman who opened her heart and home to homeless dogs is Pia Grønning, a Danish film actor who appeared in Hollywood movies in the 1970s. She still works as a model and strives to educate advertisers about using age-appropriate people for advertisements.

More than forty years ago, this lovely woman rescued a cat whom she named Musse, which was her mother's name, and a dog named Minute Maid who was a small poodle/terrier mix. Whenever she can, she speaks out about homeless animals and encourages family members, friends, colleagues, and even strangers to share their homes with strays.

Pia has always loved small dogs that she can hold on her lap and cuddle. Life with Musse and Minute Maid was very good for many years. She adored them both, and they traveled everywhere with her.

When Minute Maid passed from natural causes when she was almost twenty years old, Pia grieved. And grieved. In fact, she grieved for five years until she felt ready to rescue another dog.

Although she looked for a while, Pia just didn't feel the connection for which she was looking. Then she read about an event that was going to be held in Santa Monica, California, by a rescue organization called Perfect Pet. It was a beautiful sunny day on June 16, 1998, when Pia drove up to the shelter.

"I hoped I would find the one," Pia remembered.

As she looked at the dogs, one stood out from the rest. The little pup was a Jack Russell/Chihuahua mix and weighed about nine pounds. One of the volunteers told her the dog was about two years old and very friendly.

"I was a bit worried about her personality. Both breeds are known to be wild, and I wanted a dog that was calm, especially because of Musse's age," Pia said.

When the volunteer handed Pia the little dog, the dog was quite calm. "I was thrilled. I sat down on a chair, and she curled up in my lap as if she was home," Pia continued.

The dog was calm even though there were many people rushing around and other dogs were barking and howling for attention. In fact, she fell asleep, and Pia knew she was going home with her. In describing that first meeting, Pia said, "It was love at first sight."

After signing the adoption papers and paying $100 for the dog's vaccinations and spaying, Pia took her new addition, which she named Miss Molly, to a party to show her off. Miss Molly was the hit of the party.

"She was so well-behaved, and all the guests loved her. She went from lap to lap to lap and loved all the attention," Pia said. "Her behavior with strangers convinced me I made the right choice."

The pup was exhausted by the time they got home from the party, but perked up when Pia introduced her to Musse. Musse adopted Miss Molly instantly as her own and even gave her a kitty bath as a welcome. From that day on, Musse and Miss Molly slept together in Musse's kitty bed in Pia's bedroom.

"When I married, my husband said he favored Great Danes, but when he took one look at Miss Molly, she became Daddy's girl. When we're together, Miss Molly goes from his to my lap. I think she wants to show him she's not playing favorites," Pia continued.

When Musse passed away at the age of twenty, Pia had to console herself and Miss Molly. For the first few weeks, Molly would sleep fitfully in Musse's bed alone. "I finally had to buy a bed for her because she couldn't sleep in the bed she had shared with Musse," Pia said.

She still thinks about Minute Maid and Musse, how they lived to a very old age. However, now that Miss Molly is getting up in years, she does not want to think about what will happen when Miss Molly is no longer with them.

As Pia was holding Miss Molly, she covered her little ears and softly kissed the top of Molly's head and said, "When she is no longer with us, we would like to open our home to fostering many more dogs, but she doesn't need to know that right now."

10 Chris and Cody

The Goldens Rule

Jayni and Chevy Chase

In the past, when I'd introduce myself, I always said, "I'm Chevy Chase . . . and you're not!" It was always good for a laugh. However, people don't know the "real" Chevy. People have the habit of thinking movie stars are just like the characters they portray. They may think I'm just like Fletch, the outrageous detective; Clark Griswold from the Vacation movies; or Ty Webb from *Caddyshack*.

What they don't know about me is that my wife, Jayni, and I are the proud owners of two rescue dogs, Chris and Cody.

I've always been a big fan of Puppies Behind Bars, a prison-training program first started at the Bedford Hills Correctional Facility in Westchester County, New York, which just happens to be located in the same town where my family and I live. The program teaches inmates how to train puppies for the disabled and blind and to also raise service dogs for wounded war veterans and to become bomb-sniffing detective canines for law enforcement. In fact, Jayni and I were so moved by the good this organization does that we began holding fund-raisers for them. The money we raised helped to fund the cost of raising and training the puppies.

I received a call one day from the director of the program who said they had a beautiful fifteen-month-old male golden Labrador that had passed the tests with flying colors, but suffered from bad food allergies. This made him unable to be

placed with a person with disabilities. The director asked if we were interested in meeting the dog and possibly adopting him.

Without giving it another thought, Jayni and I agreed to see if he was a match for our family. When we arrived, the director brought out the most handsome eighty-pound golden Lab I had ever seen. He looked up with his big brown eyes as if he knew who we were. He was good-natured and the immediate connection I felt was undeniable. When the director asked if we were interested in adopting Chris, we said in stereo, "Yes!"

Chris patiently sat at my side as I signed the appropriate paperwork. At the final stroke of the pen, Chris stood up and started walking toward the door as if he knew it was official. He was part of our family now.

Chris went from a life literally behind bars, even though his mission had been an honorable one, to a life of newfound freedom. He went from a small room from where the training was held to ten acres of fabulous land on which to romp and stretch his powerful legs to their full potential. He also got a family, a real family, comprised of me, Jayni, our kids, and two other Labs, one named John (after John Belushi of *Animal House* fame) and the other, Gilda (named after Gilda Radner from my time on *Saturday Night Live*.)

He meshed immediately and all three dogs kept things lively in our household for a long time. Sadly, John and Gilda have since passed away, but Chris soon was joined by our two Westies, Georgia and Mabel.

All three dogs seem to have some type of "Chevy" radar that hones in on me as soon as I sit down on the couch. I love to make up silly rhyming jingles that amuse them. They look at me with complete adulation. Of course, Jayni tells me it's because I'm the one who feeds and plays with them the most, but I'll keep thinking it's because we have a doggy "connection."

Although Chris loves his time with our kids and other dogs, he looks forward to a certain time of the day when I walk him by his favorite lake. He knows that his girl-friends, Blanca and Nina, two chocolate Labs, will be waiting patiently with their owner. It's so cute to see them vie for his attention by either running in circles or rolling over.

About a year ago, Jayni received a phone call from her friend Kelly Gitter, who is a Manhattan real estate agent and also a huge animal rescue advocate. Kelly said she noticed a note pinned to her office bulletin board. Someone was looking for a permanent home for Cody, a ten-year-old golden Lab that had been fostered in many homes, but no one wanted to adopt. The dog's next move was going to be to the local animal shelter. Kelly knew the dog was too old to be adopted, but wanted to do something so the dog could live out his years with a great family with acres of land on which to play.

As Jayni told me about Kelly's call, I could hear the hesitancy in her voice. She knew how much Chris was attached to me and didn't want to give him any reason to be jealous. I agreed with her, but then she said, "What the heck. What's one more! We can make it work. I can't let him go to a shelter to be put down."

How could I disagree?

I can't say the two Labs' first meeting was successful, or many after that. Chris was very resentful of any attention I showed Cody, although he had no problem with sharing the rest of the family. I definitely had a challenge to overcome.

It took lots of patience, compassion, and love to reassure Chris he will always be Number 1 in my life. I have to walk and feed Chris first—always. He claims his spot next to me on the couch while Cody assumes his favorite position lying across my feet. Once Chris had asserted his alpha position and Cody acquiesced to the beta role, Chris began to warm up to our latest family member. Georgia and Mabel are content to amuse each other most of the time and stay out of their way.

Now when people see Chris and Cody running through our acreage, they say it's difficult to tell them apart, they look so much alike. However, it's easy for me. Chris is always in the lead with Cody close behind as his "wingdog."

11 Pistache

Opening Hearts and Homes

Natalie Garcia

I never considered myself a dog person, although I grew up loving animals. I discovered how much joy and love a dog can bring into one's life when I rescued an Aussie mix from a shelter. She immediately stole my heart, and I named her Maggie Mae. We were inseparable. She comforted me through bad breakups. She was with me when I left home for the first time and went to college. She kept me from feeling lonely when I moved to another state. She was my soul animal; we had an amazing bond.

Several years ago, while working for a travel company, I organized a "volunteer" trip to Mexico during which, as part of their vacation, our clients would visit and volunteer their services to local animal shelters. My employer offered to cover the cost of bringing any adopted dogs back to the States.

I already had Maggie Mae; I was a "one dog" person. However, a little spaniel retriever mix followed me around the shelter. The manager of the shelter told me the pup was found living under a taxi in Cozumel three months earlier. A volunteer at the Cozumel Humane Society brought her to the shelter and named her Pistache.

I looked down at this small dog as she looked up at me with soulful, trusting eyes. Pistache paid no attention to any of the other volunteers. She stayed at my side. When it was time to leave Mexico, I had decided to bring her back to California and foster her until I found her a good home.

Pistache quickly adjusted to Maggie Mae and American life. I house-trained

her and she learned to sit. Still, I knew this was a temporary situation. When friends invited me to drive to San Diego a week later, I packed both dogs into my car for a fun weekend to see how she would react to other people.

The weekend was fun and both dogs mixed well with my friends and their pets, too. This was encouraging. By the time we left, I knew Pistache would be able to blend into any family situation. We got an early start back to Los Angeles and during the long drive home, the dogs played in the backseat.

As I drove through Orange County, an SUV that was in the lane next to me, lost control. Everything happened so fast. The SUV hit my car on the passenger side and forced it head on into the median. It began rolling and by the time it stopped, my car was upside down. I lost consciousness.

I woke up screaming and disoriented. I had no idea where I was or how far away I was from Los Angeles. As I pulled myself from the wreck, I looked into the backseat. Both windows were shattered and the dogs were gone. Glass and dry dog food were spread all over the freeway. I went into shock. I kept asking if anyone had seen my dogs, but the emergency personnel were concentrating on treating my injuries. I was rushed to the ER in an ambulance and went reluctantly because I didn't know where my dogs were.

Before reaching the hospital, I called my partner who immediately called friends and told them what happened. By the time I was released, friends were at the scene of the accident searching for the dogs. Within a few days, we had more than a hundred volunteers searching and flyers with the dogs' pictures were posted throughout the area at shelters, vet offices, and on telephone posts.

On the fifth day, a woman called to say she had seen Pistache at a Costco near the scene of the accident. When we finally found Pistache, she was badly injured and obviously starving, thirsty, and terrified. With tears in my eyes, I picked her up cautiously. She licked my face and knew she was safe.

After an emergency visit to my vet, Pistache was safely home. My focus now was on finding my Maggie Mae. I felt so connected to her that I was convinced she would find her way to me.

We continued searching for two days until I received a call from a woman who saw our flyers. She said her father recently passed away and in a dream he told her to call and tell me to search on the other side of the river from where the search parties were looking. As I spoke to her, a seagull landed on the sidewalk in front of me. It wouldn't stop screeching or let me pass. It stopped me in my tracks. I was startled. Then it flew to the other side of the river, just as the caller had suggested.

As we reached the other side, a second seagull landed screeching in front of me just as the other gull had done. I stopped to see what this one would do. My eyes followed it as it flew to a nearby telephone pole. Just past the pole I saw the train tracks. On the tracks lay my lovely Maggie Mae. Even from a long distance away, I knew what had happened. She was gone.

In honor of Maggie's memory, I started an organization called Mae-Day and got people to volunteer at Mexican spay/neuter centers. In the past two years, we've opened our home to foster dogs privately, and have found homes for more than 150 dogs in the United States.

We now are a family with three dogs. Pistache has helped Clarence, a Chinese crested mix, and Mimsy, a dachshund/schnauzer mix, acclimate to our routine. Both were rescued from the Baldwin Park Shelter, which used to have the highest kill rate in Los Angeles County. Thankfully, through the efforts of Animal Advocate Alliance and United Hope Rescue, their adoption rate has soared.

My passion is to let people know about the joy of fostering dogs who might otherwise be put to sleep, and most importantly, finding families to love them.

Say Hey Kid

Bob Einstein

My wife, Roberta, and I love longhaired German shepherds. This is probably why we have rescued so many from the German shepherd rescue during our marriage. It is a known fact that because the AKC does not acknowledge this breed, many puppies end up in shelters, oftentimes euthanized before they can be adopted. On the other side of the coin, it is a little-known fact that longhaired shepherds are not as serious as their shorthaired counterparts. In fact, their personalities are more clownlike and comical; one might even say goofy.

I was still grieving for my dog, Teddy, who had recently passed away after a long illness. It was devastating to see him suffer. When it came time for him to leave this earth, I know he went to a better place, but I was still not ready to say good-bye.

A short time after Teddy passed, my wife received a call from the German shepherd rescue asking if we were interested in adopting another puppy.

When she spoke with me about the call, I was adamant about not going. "It's too soon, Berta. I just can't," was my immediate answer.

Berta replied, "Let's just go and see what happens, Bob. I'll let you make the decision. If you're not ready, then we won't adopt him. Okay?"

How could I say, "No," to her proposition without looking like a total jerk? I knew Berta understood my feelings so I went with my mind made up that no matter what the puppy looked like, it would not be coming home with us.

When we got to the rescue facility, I again reminded Berta that we were just going to look, not adopt, right? She nodded her head indicating a "yes" to my question so there was not going to be any misunderstanding.

We spoke with the manager, and he brought the puppy out to meet us. I tried not to make eye contact; however, I was unable to avert my eyes from the gorgeous, longhaired puppy that bounded over to me and sat down, looking straight into my eyes.

"Be strong," I shouted in my head, but my heart melted under his gaze. Berta was silent during this exchange and just watched my face turn from a set jaw to a large smile. She knew all bets were off. We were going home with a new puppy, and she didn't have to persuade me one iota.

I got off my chair and sat on the floor. The puppy curled up in my lap. It was an unnecessary move. He had me at the moment I saw his eyes that seemed to say, "Say Hey Kid!"

For those of you who are avid baseball fans, you will understand why I had to name him Willie Mays. The Say Hey Kid was his nickname. Mays was a major league player whose record some believe makes him the greatest baseball player of all time. This, of course, was before athletes got hooked on performance-enhancing drugs. He first played in the Negro League and eventually made his way into the Major Leagues. Mays was all heart and gave the fans what they wanted. He was just what this puppy showed me . . . all heart and lots of love to give. Just what I wanted.

We adopted Willie Mays that day, and Berta was smart and kind enough not to say, "I told you so," on the drive home. She just smiled at how I beamed every time I glanced over at Willie.

There is no doubt that Willie Mays is my boy. He is always at my side, and Berta says we should have named him Shadow instead of Willie Mays. To prove it, she reminds me of how every morning Willie hops into the golf cart for the ride

over to the club where everyone greets him as if he is Willie Mays. As I park the cart, voices calling, "Say Hey Kid," can be heard from members who are getting ready to tee off.

Willie brings out the best in me, and I cannot imagine my life without him. He immediately assesses my mood and knows if I need cheering up. When this happens, he will pull out one of his toys, fling it wildly into the air, jump as high as he can, and purposely miss it just to make me laugh. His goofy antics, such as when he is chasing a rabbit and lets the rabbit win the pursuit or letting a thrown stick hit him in the head, are not only heartwarming, but also bring out peals of laughter from whoever is around.

If I come home in a happy mood, Willie acts even goofier, if that's possible. He runs around my legs until he falls over because he is dizzy. When this happens, I run around and fall on the floor, too. And there we lie, two goofballs on the floor, which sends Berta into a complete laughing hysteria.

If Willie wants to go for a walk, he prances over to the closet, pulls his leash down from the hook, brings it to me, and lays it on my feet, indicating that no matter what I am doing, whether I'm taking a nap or working, he thinks we both need some outside time. "Now!" Or, if I miss his mealtime, he carries his bowl to wherever I am and drops it loudly on the floor to remind me, "It's time to feed me." His favorite antic is to wake me up by jumping on the bed, being careful not to wake Berta, of course, straddling my chest, and giving me a "juicy" good morning greeting. How can you not laugh at his communication methods? After all, they get immediate results.

Looking back to the day when Willie Mays came into my life, I cannot thank Berta enough for making me get out of the house to meet a little longhaired puppy that helped me end my grieving and showed me how to enjoy life again.

13 Buddy

Getting His Seal of Approval

Travis Mayfield

Because I'm the owner of a Next Level Fitness franchise, I arrive at the gym every day between 3:30 and 4:00 a.m. to start my day. One day during January 2012, I spotted a small, white, raggedy animal lurking around the back entrance. I couldn't tell what kind of animal it was, only that its tail was wrapped around its legs to protect it from the cold.

It looked like a large cat that ran away quickly when it saw me. My gym is in an area where coyotes hunt into the early morning hours, so I was concerned about the cat's safety. My trainers started noticing the animal hanging around as well. Each tried to catch it, but they never got close and it was too fast.

One day one of the trainers cornered the animal in the bushes and called the pound to have it picked up. Even though the city sent two animal control officers to catch it with nets, the small creature managed to get away again.

That evening, I told my wife what happened and she was concerned about the animal's safety, too.

The next morning, once again, I arrived at 3:30 a.m. The animal was about a hundred yards away and didn't run this time; it just stared at me. I crouched down and called to it, but it ran away once again. Each day, I tried to earn its trust by not chasing it, and each day, it came a little closer. By the fourth day, it came to within twenty yards; it no longer looked like a cat. Now it looked like a giant rat!

I decided to change tactics. Instead of acknowledging its presence, I turned around, opened the door, and walked into the gym. I left the door open to see if it would follow me. Sure enough, it did!

I ran out the front door, closing it behind me. I then ran to the back, through the open door, and closed it. The animal was trapped and suddenly rolled onto its back. I could finally see it was a small male dog, just skin and bones. His head was dirty and scarred, and one of his back legs was bloody.

I walked over to him slowly and was surprised he let me pick him up without any fuss. He was shaking as I wrapped him in a towel. Luckily my daughter works for a vet, so I called and the vet said to bring him.

I gently put him in the passenger seat. During the drive, he didn't move, probably wondering what was going to happen. I petted him gently to reassure him he was safe and called him "Buddy." My initial idea was to get him cleaned up and find a good home for him.

The vet said Buddy was a little over a year old and probably had been on his own for a while to have gotten into such bad shape. He told me the bill would be more than $500 just to get Buddy well enough to be put up for adoption. I didn't hesitate. I made my decision to pay the bill and take Buddy home.

My wife was quite upset when I walked in with this small, emaciated creature. We already had two cats and a female dog named Missy. However, we were relieved to see how our pets reacted to Buddy. They must have sensed Buddy had been abused and accepted him without question. At that moment, my wife knew she was outnumbered.

She got out two bowls, filled one with dog food and the other with water. Buddy ran to the food and ate every morsel and drank every drop. We were amazed Buddy ate more than our large dog.

After everyone finished their meals, my wife went to the closet and got a warm blanket for Buddy. She placed it next to Missy's blanket. Missy took to Buddy as if she were his mother. As Buddy watched, she fluffed his blanket. As I turned off the light, I was happy to see the dogs cuddled together.

However, when I awoke the next morning, my wife was sitting up with a scowl on her face pointing to the foot of our bed. Buddy had left his warm blanket and was sleeping on my legs. Her scowl turned into a smile when Buddy woke up wagging his tail, jumped onto her lap, and licked her hand.

Buddy definitely had begun to wiggle his way into my wife's heart!

Nevertheless, it took a while before she completely accepted Buddy. He wasn't house-trained and required more attention, cleanup, and love than our other pets. Yet, through it all, my wife was patient, and Buddy eventually became her favorite.

Once Buddy regained his strength, I brought him to work with me. He has accompanied me every day since then. Every trainer and every member of the gym knows Buddy, but he is very selective about who he accepts as a friend. If you get the "Buddy Seal of Approval," he will greet you at the gym door and run quickly back to my side. If you don't meet with his approval, Buddy will wedge himself between me and the other person while barking, just to let you know not to come too close to me.

It's strange how things work out; how a moment can change the lives of so many. When I found Buddy, he wasn't only starving for food, he also was starving for someone to love him—and he chose me. I never knew I could love an animal as much as I love Buddy. Buddy has become more than a pet. He has become the backbone of Next Level Fitness by showing our members what you can overcome when you put your mind to it!

The Answer to a Prayer

Sarah Jang

I had always wanted a dog, but my parents would never allow me to have one. My only childhood experience was with other people's pets and the occasional stray dog I encountered while playing outside. I had no idea of the amount of work, patience, and love that having and caring for a pet entailed.

Yet I was tired of being alone, especially during days when I was chronically ill or suffered from depression. I imagined a cute, fluffy puppy lying patiently in my lap, licking my hand, and healing my wounded spirit. I loved a neighbor's polite, well-behaved golden retriever service dog and how much it added to their family life. I would watch the children walking her and imagined it was me, smiling at the neighbors, and showing off my new dog.

One day I went online and looked at the dogs that were up for adoption at the San Diego County animal shelter. Several interested me, so I took the leap of faith and drove there with the hope I wouldn't be driving home alone.

Unfortunately, as I presented the list to the staff member at the shelter, each name was deleted, mostly because of medical issues that needed to be addressed before the dogs could be adopted. I was disappointed, but found myself asking, "Are there perhaps any other dogs you could recommend?" I told her my requirements: a nice dog, definitely friendly, and perhaps one that could be trained as a therapy dog in the future.

"Well, we do have a dog, but it might not meet all of your expectations. I don't think it would hurt for you to take a look at her," she replied.

Before she brought the dog to the foyer, she said, "The dog is an Australian kelpie mix. About six months ago, an animal control officer captured her as she was wandering on a street in Southern California. Our vet determined she was approximately a year-and-a-half old and already had a litter. She was in poor condition and had been a stray for a while, based on the vet's assessment of the many scars on her face probably from fighting with other dogs. She has scarring around her neck, probably from being tied down for long periods of time. The staff named her 'Abby' and she's friendly."

After bringing Abby to me, she continued telling the stray's story, "After several months of living here, she hadn't been adopted because she wasn't one of the 'popular' breeds. Finally a family with two young children adopted her. Less than a week later, Abby was returned to the shelter. Because no one had time to watch her, she had escaped and got pregnant again. Abby required more attention than they had time to give her."

The woman added that the shelter had her spayed while she was pregnant and the puppies were aborted. She was placed for adoption again. An active military man who lived alone adopted her. It seemed like a good fit. That is, until Abby jumped from a second floor window onto the top of his car, and ran away.

I could see Abby was scruffy, with tufts of hair sticking out in patches on her body. At first glance, I had no feeling for her. She looked like a plain dog that had a hard life. In fact, she looked like a wild dingo that had too many litters. Something told me to look deeper into Abby's eyes. A spark appeared. Or maybe it was the fact that I'm a sucker for a sad story. It didn't matter. I decided there was more to Abby than initially met my eye.

Now I'd like to say ours was a match made in heaven, but then I'd be lying. Many days I wondered what I got myself into when I brought Abby home. She didn't know how to be a good pet any more than I knew how to be a good pet owner. Abby exhibited everything I didn't want my pet to have: anxiety, nervousness, overexcitement, pulling while I tried to walk her, jumping on people and my furniture, chasing cars, making messes in the house, spilling the garbage and spreading it out on my carpeting, and destroying anything she could put into her mouth, which included her toys, bedding, leashes, household curtains, my belts, and expensive underwear.

Once while driving, she figured out how to roll down the automatic back window by hitting the button and escaped into traffic while I was stopped at a stop sign. I finally caught up with her after she had made it through a flower nursery, wagging her tail at the customers and staff. Everyone thought it was funny. Abby did, too. I, on the other hand, had a different view. After leaving the nursery, I had to chase her a block and a half before I finally cornered her and she surrendered.

After we got home, I sat down on the couch, completely exasperated and angry. I was at a point of trying to decide whether I should give up as the other people had and return her to the shelter or send her away to obedience school. Maybe Abby read my mind because instantly she jumped up on the couch, sat quietly next to me, wiggled her head under my arm, and licked my hand. After her outing, she was completely exhausted and fell asleep. So was I.

I decided that instead of reading books and asking other people about how they trained their pets, I would let Abby show me what I needed to learn. Patience. Yes, it was tested time and time again. Nevertheless, hour by hour and day by day, Abby learned to trust me, and I learned to trust my instincts as a pet owner. I showed her love balanced with a healthy dose of positive reinforcement and lots of treats when she behaved well. When she didn't, she soon learned the look of disappointment on my face meant no treats or getting to sit on my lap. Abby responded well to this new training, but it took time.

However, something else wonderful happened while I was training Abby. She learned my moods. If I begin to feel lonely, Abby is there with a wagging tail and a friendly bark. When I feel depressed, Abby lifts my spirit by grabbing her leash and taking me for a walk in the fresh air. When I am in pain, Abby sits quietly by my side, which comforts me. In the end, I got the friend I had asked God for.

15   Lola, Lucky, and Lucy

The Karmic Journey

Natasha Hofmekler

My husband and I moved our children and our cat, Weeone, from New York City to California. The first thing Weeone did was to go outside to play in the grass and flowers, and climb trees for the first time. He became adventurous and began to leave our yard to explore our neighborhood. We weren't too concerned because Weeone always came back at dusk. One evening, he didn't come home. We desperately searched our neighborhood, put up posters, asked our neighbors if they had seen him, and visited many shelters, with no results. We were all devastated.

Two weeks later, on Christmas Eve, Weeone showed up at the back door. His tail was ripped. He was dirty and starving. We surmised he must have survived a coyote attack by the looks of him. We were so happy he was safe; his homecoming was a wonderful Christmas gift.

On Christmas Day, we had our families over for a traditional holiday dinner. After we opened presents, my cousin handed me a surprise present. The huge box wiggled as I took it. I was afraid to open it. When she assured me I would love it, I did. Down at the bottom of the box was a tiny kitten. She thought the kitten would help with our loss, as she did not know Weeone had come home the night before.

We named him Boots because of his white paws. Boots grew up to be quite handsome and wandered the neighborhood as Weeone did, except he was not climbing trees. He was looking for females. One night, he didn't come back.

Again, we were devastated. We did everything we had done when Weeone had disappeared. We also went through hundreds of pictures of rescued cats on the Internet. A month later, we saw a cat that looked just like Boots. When we visited the shelter, we were disappointed because it wasn't Boots. He was a feral cat that was going to be euthanized later that day. We agreed to adopt him.

When we finished completing the adoption papers, we decided to take a look at the pit bull section, knowing these dogs have the least chance of being adopted.

I saw a skinny American Staffordshire caged with five other pits. She obviously had been attacked by them. She was lying on her back in submission and clearly couldn't fight anymore. We couldn't leave her in that situation and decided to add her to our family. I named her Lola. My husband walked Lola, and I carried Junior, the feral cat, to our car.

Lola was in bad shape. She was shivering, coughing, and her nose was running. When we took her to our veterinarian, he said she had pneumonia and kennel cough. He told us she was lucky we adopted her because she wouldn't have lived much longer in those conditions.

We cared for Lola as if she were a sick child. She slept with us. She was so small for a five-month-old puppy, so we put her in warm sweaters and wrapped her in soft blankets. We gave her food fortified with steamed carrots, celery, and premium whey.

Lola recovered and was growing up to be an amazing dog: lean, energetic, fast, and agile. However, we could tell she was lonely; she wanted another dog to play with.

We were thinking we should go back to the shelter where we adopted her. In the meantime, we took Lola for her training session at the Canyon View Training Ranch in Malibu, a wonderful five-acre training facility for canines. Manuel, her trainer, told us another trainer brought Lucky, a pit bull/Jack Russell mix, to the ranch that morning after she found him at a shelter the evening before Lucky was to be euthanized. She got him out of there and brought him to the ranch to work with him and find him a home. The dog had been abandoned as a puppy and grew up on the mean streets of Los Angeles, barely surviving terrible abuse, starvation, and disease. Lucky appeared to be suffering from post-traumatic stress syndrome. He was aggressive toward people in uniform, particularly mailmen and UPS drivers. Manuel said this aggression scared people, so there wasn't much chance for him to be adopted. He and Lola seemed to get along, so we decided to bring Lucky home on a trial basis.

We knew the dog deserved to have a loving home and good life. When our son, Nehemiah, met Lucky, there was a deep connection. They hugged and kissed each other as if they were long-lost brothers who had found each other again. It took a while for Lucky to realize we loved him and wouldn't hurt him. Now he and Lola run and play in the grass, chasing each other back and forth.

We were so grateful that Manuel brought Lucky to us. Manuel is such a wonderful trainer and good-hearted animal lover we decided to hire him to care for Lucky and Lola full-time.

After adopting Lucky, we decided to purchase the property next to ours. With more land, we knew we could adopt another dog. One morning a black-and-white pit bull puppy named Lucy was featured on the news. She needed a home and was at Karma Rescue waiting to be adopted. Karma Rescue saves at-risk dogs from high-kill shelters in Los Angeles. When we arrived at the rescue we saw so many wonderful dogs available for adoption. The manager told us that Lucy was a big puppy and probably would grow up to be a very large dog. Most people want smaller dogs, so the fact we showed up to see her was probably destiny.

Lucy is the poster girl of how wonderful pit bulls can be. She is a beautiful, gentle giant with a puppy mentality who loves to play with squeaky toys and play tug-of-war with the other dogs (she always wins). If none of them want to play, Lucy finds ways to amuse herself, either by digging in the yard or running around in circles or patrolling the fence hoping to find a squirrel or bird to chase out of the yard.

We knew we could do more to help.

We were inspired to launch a new line of nutritional products for pets, using high-grade, natural ingredients, the same type with which we nurtured Lola back to good health. We believe good nutrition is the basis of a pet's health. Our pets are proof of this. Weeone is a healthy twelve-year-old cat who is limber and still climbs trees easily. Junior, at almost eighteen years old, still plays like a kitten and even occasionally tries to catch mice on our property.

We became an extended family with two children, three dogs, and two cats—and enough love to go around. We often talk about destiny and how it played a large role in leading us to each of these wonderful animals.

16 Teddybear, Darby, Maizie, and Lovey

Always Room for One More

Laurie and Peter Marshall

One Friday, Peter and I decided that although we already had two cats, we wanted to adopt a terrier, our favorite breed. This was our intention when we went to the Lange Foundation animal rescue in West Los Angeles. As we looked at the dogs in the cages, Peter spotted this little chow who looked about three months old. The moment we approached, he came to the front of his cage and looked at us with his soft sad eyes. He had a deep cut around his neck. The manager said the dog's former owner had tied a string around the dog's neck and, as he grew, the string cut into it. A neighbor reported the abuse to the authorities and the dog was removed from the home. The string had to be surgically removed.

Peter wanted to adopt him, but I was reluctant. I told him I heard chows were mean and wouldn't touch him. Peter picked him up and handed him to me. I could tell quickly that the dog was a gentle soul that wasn't bitter about his treatment by his former owner. He was so fluffy. As I petted him, I called him, "My little Teddybear." That became his name.

Teddybear fit right into the pace of our household. He followed us around; in fact, so much so that Peter suggested it might be nice for Teddybear to have a playmate to keep him occupied when we were busy. I saw a video on Facebook of

two blond chows, a male and female, that volunteers at a South Los Angeles pound had posted, hoping to spark some interest.

By this time, I knew chows made great pets, so I went to see them. When I arrived, the manager said the dogs had been transferred to a rescue shelter, but would not tell me where. I don't know why, but it seemed as if many of the people who were working there seemed uncompassionate . . . not at all what you would hope for when thinking about the caring these animals need.

It took two months of me calling shelters before I finally located the dogs at the Bill Foundation. When we saw them, the male was friendly and took to us right away. The female was older and seemed depressed, withdrawn. The manager said she had been badly abused by her former male owner and the details were too horrible to share. We decided to foster the male to see how he and Teddybear would get along. The boys took to each other immediately, but the new chow was rough with our cats so we had to take him back.

Peter suggested we take Darby, the female, to foster. I had absolutely no connection with her. By this time, she was being fostered at a vet's office. When I saw her looking so sad in the crate, I agreed to foster her with the stipulation they continue looking for a home for her.

By Saturday, we realized Darby hated men. She growled at Peter, warning him to keep his distance, and wanted nothing to do with Teddybear. As much as she hated Peter, she loved me. By the second day, Darby adopted me as her mother.

She would snuggle up to me when I sat on the couch reading. She would follow me around the house and sat by my side as if to protect me when Peter and I spoke. Peter thought it was cute. The first time he asked, "Where's your momma?" Darby ran over and bumped her head into my leg. This stole my heart.

I called the rescue shelter and told them it might be best for them to find Darby a home with no males or other pets. Peter overheard my conversation and said we couldn't send her back. She had been through so much. I was so relieved, and Darby became my dog.

Later that evening, I attended a funeral for a golf buddy in Manhattan Beach. I became depressed as I drove home and made a quick stop at the Carson pound to say "hello" to the animals the way you would stop by an old folks' home to cheer up the residents.

This was not a rescue shelter. Dogs are euthanized after ten days if no one adopts them. I saw an old little ratty mop of a dog that had something special about her. I was told her name was Maizie, but her time was up and she was

scheduled to be put down the following day. There were so many cute little dogs, she had no chance of being chosen. I told them I would adopt her.

Maizie had to be spayed first so I couldn't get her until Monday. I asked if they could shave her dirty fur before they operated. They said they wouldn't have time and didn't seem to care.

When I came home from the funeral and told Peter that by Monday we would be a three-dog family, he was surprised, but said, "What's one more?"

All I could think of on Sunday was that Maizie would probably get an infection from the surgery. I prayed she would be all right.

When I picked her up on Monday evening, I saw she had been shaved. I was so happy that I cried. I am sure they thought I was weird, but I knew she had a better chance of healing.

When I saw her face, I realized she wasn't an old dog. She had the most beautiful young puppy face that had been hidden by the dirty, matted fur. I fell in love at second sight.

Three years later, Peter and I were discussing how, in one weekend, we went from having no dogs to adopting three. We still donate pillows, blankets, and dog beds to the Lange Foundation and bring Teddybear to visit.

On one visit, we made the mistake of walking through to see the dogs. A little, monkey-looking dog with its head tilted to one side caught our eye at the same time. The manager told us she had been there six weeks. No one would adopt her because she had a neurological problem that caused her head to droop and she stumbled when she walked.

Peter and I looked at each other and said simultaneously, "What's one more?" We named her Lovey because she is, well, lovey.

We used to travel a lot. However, we have more entertainment at home than we could imagine any place could offer. It's our happiest place on earth.

17   Rémy Martin

Bringing Smiles to Everyone

M. Michele Martin

After the chaos of the Christmas holidays, I resolved on January 1, 2011, to make my life mean something more instead of just focusing on my usual resolutions of losing weight and exercising. I gave it a lot of thought. I decided to share my good life with a dog; not just any dog, but one that needed to be rescued.

The next day, I called Carole Sax, my friend who volunteers with a rescue group called Animal Alliance. When I told her of my New Year's resolution, she was thrilled because so many animals are in need of adoption. She asked if I wanted a male or female, large or small or in-between, a puppy, or full-grown dog. I really did not have any particular type of dog in mind. I told her that my only parameter was that the dog be friendly.

Carole called within a week and said, "I have found the perfect dog for you. She's a white female Lhasa apso mix and is as cute as a button, but you have to get here quickly."

I met Carole at the Animal Alliance where I learned more about the dog's history. The dog had been picked up by an animal control officer in an affluent section of Los Angeles called Baldwin Hills. Carole said the dog had no tags so there was no way to contact her family. The shelter where she was taken is a kill facility, which means if a dog is not adopted within seventy-two hours after its arrival, it is euthanized. The Alliance rescued the dog from the shelter just a few hours before she would have lost her life.

Carole brought the dog out to meet me, and my heart ached for this small, undernourished animal. She was obviously frightened and her soulful eyes looked up at me as if to say, "Please love me."

I got down on both knees and called to her. Without hesitation, the dog jumped into my arms and snuggled her small head under my arm as if she was seeking safety. I fell in love with her in an instant.

I brought her home, and we began the New Year with different, and better, lives. Because my last name is Martin, I decided to call her Rémy, after the fine French cognac. This suits her because she has an air of sophistication about her.

The last two years with Rémy have been amazing. From the moment she came into my life, she has showered me with love, which told me she had never been abused. My five-year-old niece loves playing with Rémy. As they roll on the floor, Rémy smothers her with doggy kisses.

I realized Rémy had a lot of love to give. Because she was given a second chance in life, I wanted to think of a way for her to "pay it forward." It didn't take long before I found the perfect solution.

Since I am a volunteer at Cedars-Sinai Medical Center in Los Angeles, I know there is always a great need for therapy dogs to visit patients and their families. I did some research and quickly took the first step. I enrolled in The Pet Partners' Therapy Animal Handler Course, an eight-hour workshop that concentrated on the "human" end of the leash taught at the Delta Organization. I learned what was required for Rémy and me to become a great therapy team.

The course covered things like preparing for visits, identifying stress in Rémy and how to de-stress her, animal health and safety, the dog's interaction with different types of people, and different facilities' health and safety codes. After taking several written tests, I completed the course with flying colors.

Afterward, I made an appointment to have Rémy evaluated, which consisted of an intensive one-and-a-half-hour assessment with a counselor. During this time, the counselor tested Rémy to see if she was controllable and predictable. Rémy also had to prove she had good social skills and reacted well to strangers. The counselor said Rémy passed the evaluation easily and that we would make a great team. I knew at that moment that this year was going to be special.

That was a year ago.

Now we visit the hospital every other week. Rémy patiently allows me to attach her hospital photo ID badge to her collar. The moment I grab her leash, it is difficult for her to contain her excitement; somehow she knows where we're going. She proudly leads me into the hospital with her badge around her neck for all to see. After greeting the reception staff, who always has homemade doggy treats, Rémy and I make the rounds to visit patients in their rooms, beginning with the children who are recovering from surgery. They adore her visits. Rémy allows them to pet and snuggle with her. Some have even had their parents bring doggy toys to play with in their rooms.

After the patient visits, we turn our attention to family members who are waiting for their loved ones while they are in surgery. Somehow Rémy senses the great stress these people are under. She slowly approaches each one and waits until they acknowledge her presence, usually by them rubbing her head or back. Rémy gives them a moment of distraction and helps to relieve the tension. I have witnessed small miracles as Rémy lies on the floor next to seated family members who find great comfort in the love she shows them just by being there. In a moment, their tears turn to smiles as she puts her paw on their hands, as if to let them know she is there for them in their time of worry.

It took the Rémy Martin brand more than three hundred years to build a reputation of quality and foster a legacy of being a benchmark for other liquors to attain. It took my Rémy Martin just one year to build her reputation of the "dog that brings a smile to everyone she sees" and set a standard of what unconditional love really is.

Otis, Donni, Breaker, and Lulu

Angels Who Walk Among Us

Michelle Neufeld Montak

Sarah McLachlan wrote a beautiful song called "Angel." The song is about second chances for those who are at the bottom, and that those poor souls are being saved by an angel. When you think about the horrible life many homeless animals experience, these words could apply to them.

Michelle Neufeld Montak, founder of Gimme Shelter Animal Rescue based out of New York, is such an angel. She became involved after witnessing the incredibly inhumane treatment of animals in kill shelters, mainly in the South.

She rescues these dogs and finds them loving comfort, in forever homes. However, she not only finds homes, she has also taken in four dogs herself.

"I watched Otis being born almost fifteen years ago in a local shelter. His mother was a stray that was picked up just before she gave birth to her litter on a damp, cold floor in the dark. I knew the puppies only had seven days for someone to walk into the shelter and adopt them," she recalled.

One little guy had gray-and-white fur. His puppy eyes were hidden behind gray tufts of wild hairs. "I named him Otis and took him to my vet who cared for him until he was old enough for me to bring home. Opening my home and heart to him put me on the path of helping other homeless dogs," Michelle remembered. "I always joke that Otis is a person . . . but actually I have come to realize over the years with Otis, that he is WAY better than any human could ever be. He is kind, gentle, and loving. He is my heart, my soul, my everything. He has such a quiet quality. It is as if he knows what I'm thinking. He bounces around when I'm happy and sits silently at my side when I'm troubled. I cannot imagine the world without my Otis."

Their deep connection is the epitome of unconditional love and trust.

The shelter in which Otis was born was a five-star hotel compared to what Michelle found when she began visiting kill centers in North and South Carolina.

She visited one more than four years ago that was converted from an old jail in Marlboro, North Carolina. It was unfit for hardened criminals, yet city officials deemed the facility good enough for homeless dogs. They crammed twenty-five dogs into five-foot-by-ten-foot jail cells, and the dogs lived in those jail cells in two inches of standing sewer water. The stench of open wounds, infections, urine, and feces permeated the air. The dogs were filthy and starving. Their days were numbered.

Michelle spotted a brown, black, and white puppy with floppy ears that looked like she wanted to ask a question. She was so fearful and sad and would not allow anyone to touch her except Michelle. She remembered, "It almost seemed as if she looked into my soul and asked, 'Why don't you take me home?'" Since she already had Otis, she told the shelter she would foster the puppy, which she named Donni. She was afraid that Otis and Donni might not get along because of the puppy's personality.

"I was happy when I was proven wrong," Michelle said. "Once home, Donni's fear left quickly. They got along beautifully. I believe Otis was glad to have another playmate besides me. I refer to her as the foster dog that never left."

A year later, Gimme Shelter conducted a rescue mission at the Chesterfield, South Carolina, facility, a known kill center. The staff euthanize dogs after a week if they aren't adopted. Four golden retriever/German shepherd mix puppies about three months old were housed next to the gas chamber waiting their turn. These puppies were transported to Michelle's shelter in the hopes of finding foster and/or forever homes.

"The second I saw this big-pawed, gorgeous hunk of a guy, something clicked. I knew he was going to be mine. He had a wonderful presence about him; however, I had a hard time convincing my husband, Eddie, to let me bring home a third dog, even on a foster basis," Michelle said. "Once my husband saw the bond that had already formed between the dog and me, I knew he wouldn't say 'no.' I named him Breaker because he is such a heartbreaker. He is my gentle giant and a big goof." Michelle compares Breaker to Matthew McConaughey; so gorgeous, but he doesn't seem to know it.

Approximately six months later, Michelle visited the Chesterfield shelter again. She was told six days prior to her visit that a driver had seen a sack full of something being thrown from a moving car. When the driver stopped to investigate, he found puppies in extremely bad condition in the sack. Someone had left the puppies to die in a ditch. By the time the person brought them to the shelter, only one had survived and she was extremely sick.

Michelle added, "Even though someone thought she and her brothers and sisters were little more than garbage to be tossed aside without another thought, I saw a special creature that does not have a mean bone in her body. The first things I noticed were her kind eyes shining brightly on her black furry face. She was very weak, and she let me hold her while the vet treated her. I think she is a mix of Labrador and Newfoundland. Even though she has a tough exterior, she is as mushy as melted butter on the inside. I called her Lulu. She is a survivor."

To date, Gimme Shelter has saved upward of two thousand animals. Michelle concluded, "My hope is these stories will educate readers about the importance of spaying and neutering their dogs, and about the thousands and thousands of homeless animals in this country. I hope readers are inspired to open their hearts and give abandoned animals loving, permanent homes."

The Little Dog with the Big Name

Logan Holzman

Hurricane Katrina hit the residents of New Orleans hard in 2005. Eventually, they were able to dig out and get relief from our government and many nonprofits.

However, what happened to the pets that suddenly became homeless is another story. Thank God for organizations like Madalin's Used Dogs Rescue. Its founder, Madalin Laurie Bernard, was in the midst of the chaos as the military stepped in to stop the looting and shootings. She started rescuing dogs before the winds died down.

She knew she couldn't do it alone. As the word spread about the work she was doing saving the lives of so many pets, volunteers showed up in droves. Logan Holzman was one of those special people.

She was a student at Tulane University and even though she carried a full load of classes, she always made sure she had time to donate her services.

A week after Katrina hit, Logan's boyfriend, Mike, was driving through a residential neighborhood on his way home when he saw a starving dog eating garbage. The dog was very skinny and completely covered in scabs and bleeding sores. The dog let Mike wrap him up in his jacket and carry him to the backseat of his car. He didn't have the strength to resist.

Mike called Logan to ask if he could bring home a stray that was in pretty bad shape. They had just finished fostering a litter of puppies and were looking forward to some quiet time before they took in another dog.

It was difficult to imagine what these animals went through during the aftermath of the hurricane. They had lost their masters and were thrown into a world of uncertainty, not knowing where their next meal, if any, would come from. They were homeless. Afraid. Starving. Of course she said, "Yes."

"I had no idea what to expect, but nothing could have prepared me for the sight of this dog. His skin looked like it was draped over his bones. I had experience with mange, but this dog's entire body was infested and the only fur he had left was a small tuft on the tip of his tail," Logan explained.

Mike carried him to her porch and Logan immediately called a vet. They gave him food that he ate in huge gulps. He drank the water as quickly as he could. "He looked at us with such sad eyes and wagged his tail slowly. My heart broke for this poor creature," Logan said.

She knelt down to pet him and realized that under the dirt and crust on his neck was a black leather collar. This used to be someone's pet.

The vet treated the dog, which Logan named Willis. His picture and story was distributed through Madalin's network and Logan agreed to foster him for as long as it took to find a forever home for him.

When Logan first brought Willis home, he stayed in his crate all the time and only came out when he had to go potty or eat.

Yet in a relatively short period of time, Willis's condition improved drastically. Logan remembered, "Willis's wrinkly body began to fill out. His gray-and-white fur began to grow back. His spirit and energy underwent a complete transformation. Of course, he was still afraid during storms."

Within a week, he became a typical curious young dog and never sat still. He barked when he was hungry or wanted to play. After two months, Willis found a forever home with a loving family.

In late January 2010, Logan received a phone call that her friend Sule had died suddenly in a terrible car accident. She left for Houston, Texas, the next day to be with Sule's family and attend his funeral.

In their garage was a box with Sule's dog Sophie and her two puppies for which he had been trying to find homes. The Chihuahua/poodle mix puppies were so tiny, and only about eight weeks old.

Sule's mom, Jennifer, explained the puppies' father had run away. Logan offered to take one of them home. On the drive home, she named the three-pound puppy aptly enough, Houston. At first he was calm, but during the middle of the trip, he became a wild dog, running back and forth across the seats and jumping to and from the backseat. She wondered if she had made a mistake in taking the puppy. It took Logan a little while to realize he had drunk an entire cup of her coffee while she wasn't paying attention. Thankfully, once the caffeine wore off, he became calm again. In fact, he slept for most of the way home.

About a week later, Logan called to see how Jennifer and the rest of her family were doing. She also asked if she had been able to find homes for Sophie and the other puppy. Jennifer said both had run away. Logan felt horrible, "I so wish now I had taken the mother and the other puppy, too!"

She had four female roommates, so Houston received lots of attention. They volunteered to take him on walks and played with him all the time. Logan said, "The only problem they had with Houston was that he stole their underwear, ripped them into shreds, and proudly brought them back to them as gifts."

Houston had become her sorority club's mascot and was a big hit during happy hour at Logan's favorite restaurant.

After graduating, Logan moved back to New York City and took a position with her father's company, Charitybuzz.

"Houston rides in his little papoose with his head sticking out with me on the subway when I go to work," she said.

At work, he lays on his little bed next to her desk in her office. When he wants some playtime, he goes into her father's office and plays with Biggie, her father's dog. "Of course, he's such a momma's boy, he never lets me out of his sight," Logan added.

On weekend mornings, you can find Logan and Houston on a leisurely walk through the park. He loves everyone, and everyone loves him.

She summed up by saying, "This scruffy little dog with the big name who loves string cheese is the best thing that ever happened to me."

Loved Hounds and Heroes

Tamar Geller

Tamar Geller is a well-known trainer/life coach for dogs and their owners. Her innovative, loving techniques have made her one of the most sought-out dog trainers in the country. Some of her clients have included celebrities like Oprah Winfrey, Ben Affleck, Owen Wilson, Ellen DeGeneres, Hilary Swank, Natalie Portman, Goldie Hawn, and a host of others.

Preferring the term "life coach" to "dog trainer," and "well-mannered" to "obedient," she provides insight to millions of dog enthusiasts nationwide as the resident dog expert on the *Today* show.

Tamar became interested in dogs as she watched them being trained while serving as an intelligence officer with the elite Israeli Army Special Forces. After finishing her service, she had the extraordinary opportunity to study wolves in their natural habitat, observing that they taught their young primarily through games. Concluding that a dog possesses aspects of both a wolf and a human toddler, Tamar created her innovative and revolutionary approach to dog training, an approach that is light-years ahead of the typical dog trainer pack.

Tamar also started an outreach program, called "Operation Heroes and Hounds" that help shelter dogs as well as wounded members of the armed forces. Operation Heroes and Hounds presents injured members of the U.S. military with the unique opportunity of coaching and living with shelter dogs. The focus of the program is on personal transformation through The Loved Dog™ method.

Operation Heroes and Hounds participants include "the walking wounded" of the U.S. military who suffer from nonvisible ailments, such as post-traumatic stress disorder and traumatic brain injury. Shelter dogs selected for the program are in need of behavior modification through the kind, nonaggressive teaching of The Loved Dog methods. Together, they can heal their emotional wounds while gaining new life skills.

On Board to Forever

Lisa Blodgett

Angels, angels come fast," Priscilla would have been saying if she knew her fate and the fate of her ten puppies. And the angels came bearing gifts for all. Do you think that dogs can speak to the angels in ways that we can't? This story will make you think so.

Modern technology is amazing. Just think, we can talk to a community that is like-minded, that sees our heartfelt need, with people that we have never met, with a keystroke on our computers. This is what a volunteer did, and she found other angels. Priscilla's sory is living proof of the power of the online community.

Priscilla is a soft-brown pit bull that got scooped up off the streets in Southern California, and no collar meant no home or safe haven. Fortunately, the animal shelter that she ended up in is closed now. You see, it was a kill shelter, so this was no safe haven for Priscilla, either. And, Priscilla, sweet soul, was pregnant with puppies and birthing her pups there meant that they wouldn't get the care they needed to survive.

This filled Andrea, the young volunteer at the shelter, with terror. Andrea had a soft heart, and was moved by the drama that was unfolding.

What she could do was to write a plea on Facebook with pictures that she took of Priscilla, hoping someone would see Priscilla's inner beauty, beyond a terrible skin condition—for someone to please, please take Priscilla to someplace where she could have her pups.

A woman responded and quickly got Priscilla out the front door of the shelter and into her car for a speedy getaway . . . this was as far as she could think to solve the problem for the moment.

Meanwhile, while Andrea had been going home at night and posting on Facebook about Priscilla and her plight, and that having her puppies in the shelter would be a tragedy in the making, another angel named Lisa Blodgett started reading the chronicle. Lisa saw pictures of the pregnant pup, and she feared for Priscilla. Lisa had rescued many dogs herself, and has fostered and found homes for many dogs. She was on alert, and worried.

She said, "I breathed a sigh of relief when I learned on the social media page that a really kind person stepped up to the plate to foster Priscilla, only hours before she had her babies." Her prayers were answered.

At least she thought so. But Priscilla weighed heavy on her mind. "I wanted to trust that Priscilla and her puppies were safe," said Lisa. But something stirred inside her to tell her otherwise. Where was the call for help coming from? Lisa anxiously watched the Facebook page, but it showed nothing.

And a month later, there it was. Andrea posted that Priscilla and the pups really needed a new landing. A second post said that another connected soul had said that she would take the puppies and Momma, but they would have to live outside, and in the desert—that meant 110 degrees in the day and very cold temperatures at night. Lisa panicked—they would not survive.

Up early the next morning, Lisa had a mission. She got her car ready so that she and her friend Diana could jump into service. She prepared the crates for Priscilla and her puppies, and thought about her resources and years of experience that she could offer to come to their aid.

Lisa was very concerned when she got to the home of the sweet soul who had given what she could to help Priscilla and the pups. Having just had a baby herself, the dogs were more than she could handle. Priscilla's skin condition had not gotten better, and the pups had hair loss from rashes. The pups weren't getting enough nourishment and were lethargic. All were alive, but more care was needed.

Lisa quietly carried the dogs to her car. She immediately called Desert Dunes Animal Hospital, and the angels there said that they would fit her in, as Lisa recounted the condition of Momma and her pups. Many medications and bags of puppy food and treats traveled out the front door of the clinic for the safekeeping of Lisa's charges.

Lisa had three rescue dogs herself, and now they were a family of fifteen—Lisa and fourteen scrambling, hungry, and, well, you know the rest, lovable dogs. Lisa called in the troops, dear friends, who helped bathe, feed, and medicate the new arrivals. These sweet souls who hopped on the program right away said, "This is fun, how often do we get to play with ten new puppies!" Lisa was grateful that her husband was out of town to miss the circus!

The puppies got special baths, and much love to heal them inside and out. They greatly improved, gained weight, and grew healthy. And Lisa thought about the next step. From her fostering days, she knew other angels, The Wings of Rescue pilots that fly dogs from high-kill regions at their own expense to regions where adoptable pets are in demand. It was time to call these troops to the rescue. Lisa imagined a happy long-term home for each of her sweet canine babies. Her vision was on the march, thankfully.

Priscilla and her pups were going on the next mission flight to Calgary and Alberta, Canada. Happiness abounded, and Lisa posted pictures of the pups on Facebook and the network of Wings of Rescue rolled into action. Lisa said, "I hoped no one could resist adopting my adorable pups!" Without proof of adoption, the dogs would not be allowed to enter Canada.

The three largest dogs got adopted immediately, but Lisa was on pins and needles for the rest. Another problem was that the rules stipulated that the puppies had to have someone on the plane to accompany them. Luckily, another Facebook post after someone that Lisa had not known previously, showed up. Priscilla's story inspired a sweet soul from Canada to fly to the United States and chaperone all the dogs to their new homes.

Unfortunately, the four smallest puppies didn't make it through their health certificate exam, and that meant that Olive, Pierre, Pebbles, and Charlie would not be traveling this time.

Five of the puppies traveled on the Wings of Rescue flight, and arrived safely at new homes.

Another angel, Kristin—a vet tech at the Desert Dunes Animal Hospital—asked to adopt the sixth puppy that was supposed to be on that flight. The vet tech named the puppy Abram, and Abram is currently going through the service dog program to become a therapy dog. He loves to go to work with his new momma, and he loves the attention he gets there from the staff and the veterinarian who had given him puppy love and life.

Lisa saw her dream come true with Abram and her five safely placed pups. The four puppies she was still fostering, Olive, Pierre, Pebbles, and Charlie got better, and seats were reserved for them on the next Wings of Rescue flight to Bellingham, Washington, the following month.

Olive has since been adopted by Bekki, founder of Rescued Hearts Northwest. Cait, Bekki's teenage daughter, fell in love with Olive and renamed her Stella. As Cait's puppy, Stella shadows her everywhere. Bekki's cat, Jazzy, is Stella's best friend. Stella loves running free by the lake where they live, where she can walk to the edge of the water and put one paw in.

Pierre, the runt of the litter, was adopted by a young couple, who also have a five-year-old pit bull. They have become best friends. The couple named him Jaxson and adore him as a child of their family. He still has some skin rashes, and his new vet found that he was allergic to chicken, so they changed his diet.

Pebbles was finally adopted by a family in Kent, Washington. Her parents say that they have to watch the neighbors who threaten to steal Pebbles because she is a doll!

And Charlie was adopted during the flight to Bellingham by a dog trainer who saw the picture of Charlie on the Internet. Charlie's new momma greeted him at the airport with a bag of toys, a new blanket, treats, a slicker raincoat, and lots of hugs! He is a true California dog adjusting to the rain in Washington, in his happy new home.

Priscilla resides in Canada with her new loving family who renamed her Jade. She loves playing in the snow. Her mom, Yvonne, bought her snow boots, but Jade is still trying to get used to them. Yvonne says, "It doesn't get much better than this, it's like Jade has always been a part of our family and we love her so much!"

This story of Priscilla and her ten puppies has a happy ending, but it took a village to make it happen . . . a village of angels.

Laughter Heals the Broken Heart

Tyra Golter

I had lots of love in my life. A wonderful man who I was planning to marry loved me. I had four loving pets that were all rescues. I was extremely happy and couldn't imagine my life getting any better.

I never thought that within two years, my "perfect" life would be destroyed. My boyfriend died in a horrific accident. I was still grieving when I had to cope with losing my four beloved pets during the next twelve months.

My heart was completely broken. I shut down to protect myself from any more heartbreak. For the first time in my life, I had no one or no pet to love. Slowly, depression consumed my days. I became a shell of a person and didn't want to leave home. My nights were spent tossing and turning and crying. I lost interest in things that used to bring me pleasure. I went through the motions of living and survived by not feeling. My friends worried because I became a recluse, protecting my heart by not opening it to anyone or anything. I thought, "Why bother going out when I know I won't enjoy myself?" I didn't want to ruin my friends' good time. It was easier just to refuse any invitations.

During this time, I kept seeing people walking beautiful blond or apricot-colored labradoodles. I was drawn to their easygoing and smart personalities.

When the owners gave me permission to approach their pets, I loved touching their soft, curly fur. Every one of them also verified what I had already determined: Their dogs were a pleasure to own.

However, I wasn't ready. It took two years of emptiness before I could think about getting another pet. Of course, during that time it fleetingly crossed my mind that if I were to get another pet, I would love to have a labradoodle. Yet I believed this new "designer breed" didn't fit my only criteria of getting a pet: All of mine had always been rescues.

It was the first day of spring, a day of new beginnings, when I decided to tell my friends that I was finally ready to adopt another dog. Two weeks later, a close friend told me she found the one! A woman she knew was fostering a dog and it was a blond labradoodle. I was so excited I couldn't wait for the foster mom to bring him to my home.

I opened the door expecting to see the type of dog I had seen for two years, a beautifully groomed, healthy dog. The dog that stood timidly behind her was so skinny you could count his ribs. He looked sickly and abused. His fur was thin and dull. He looked more like a starving lamb than what I imagined.

The woman explained the dog was a victim of a bad divorce. The couple's only focus was on getting out of their marriage; not taking care of their pet. They were literally starving him to death. He was two years old and weighed only forty-seven pounds, almost half the weight he should have been.

He had been adopted two times, but always returned because he had a few "bad habits." He was nervous and had "accidents" in the house. He didn't know how to play and cowered in the corner. He wasn't good around children or other dogs because he hadn't been socialized well.

He looked so broken and alone and sad. He reminded me of myself in the not-too-distant past.

She said his name was Bart. I walked over to him and gently rubbed his back. He responded well to my touch. When I whispered his name, his eyes met mine.

He didn't know "sit" or "stay," but had a funny way of tilting his head when I said his name that made me laugh.

I agreed to take him.

It was touch and go at first. Bart obviously hadn't been disciplined and he felt he had the run of the house—nothing was off-limits. He marked his territory when I wasn't looking, especially on my custom-made curtains. He had a habit of rummaging through the trash and scattering it around. He didn't play with his toys, but thought chewing on my shoes was a fun thing to do when he was bored. He wasn't used to walking with a leash and used to pull me down the street chasing anything that caught his eye. He dug up the plants in my yard and proudly placed them on my bed as a gift—roots, dirt, and rocks.

Yes, Bart had a lot of bad habits, but he had so much more to offer on the plus side. He made me laugh at his funny antics. For example, when he was tired, he would flop down anywhere and go to sleep, even if we were in the middle of a walk. He would fluff his bed by rolling it across the living room floor until it was just perfect and then circled around it about ten times before he lay down. He would bury his treats under the throw rugs instead of eating them right away. He likes to play hide-and-seek, but always hides in the same place. My favorite, though, is how he wakes me up every morning. Just before my alarm goes off, I hear Bart stretch on his bed before he jumps onto mine and then licks my face just as the alarm goes off. Sometimes I wonder if he knows how to tell time.

It took several months before Bart attained his present weight of seventy pounds. His blond, curly fur now shines, and he loves getting groomed. He watches me brush him in the full-length mirror as if admiring his studly good looks. When I'm finished, he takes his brush and puts it on the kitchen counter, then trots back to me as if he's a show dog in the ring.

His bad habits are a thing of the past, but his ability to make me laugh grows every day. He has made me feel alive again; my heart is full of joy. In reality, this rescue dog rescued me.

Prisoners of Profit

Amanda Hearst

We all come from somewhere. It is easy to forget this in our fast-paced, in-the-moment lives. With consumerism, the rush of experiencing it all, and being overwhelmed by so much at our fingertips, we may not see the whole story.

Take Amanda Hearst, for instance. Her grandfather was newspaper mogul William Randolph Hearst. She was born to philanthropist and socialite Anne Hearst, and she is an editor at *Marie Claire* magazine in New York and founder of Friends of Finn, an organization dedicated to stopping the inhumane treatment of dogs in puppy mills.

Our start in life informs our future. And that start can have a big impact on our lives in all kinds of ways, including health, opportunity, and the love that we find.

Many of us suffer from something called " shiny object" syndrome these days, which is that ready impulse that causes us to want and buy what attracts our attention. We see something new and we want it; a hot pair of shoes like Amanda writes about in her work for the magazine; something our friends have, like a cute puppy that they got from the local pet store; or the green drink that is touted to keep us healthy.

But well-trained to buy as we are, consumerism does not often tell all of the facts. Ninety-nine percent of the dogs that are sold in local pet stores come from puppy mills. That's right. You didn't know that, did you? And neither did Amanda when she got Finnegan, her beloved dachshund/Chihuahua mix. She just wanted a puppy. And she and her friends can afford to buy them, not really giving a thought about where they come from.

The local pet stores often falsely claim that their sweet puppies do not come from puppy mills. You may even see that they offer pure-bred papers from a prestigious-sounding kennel club. And as part of the marketing, you may get a health certificate, which may only be backed by a cursory wellness check.

None of this means that this little puppy caged at the local pet store does not have genetic problems or that its parents are healthy or treated humanely. "A puppy sold at a pet store," Amanda said, "keeps the puppy mills in business. They sell one and quickly get another to keep the storefront windows full to attract customers, and this is the business of mistreating and overbreeding dogs for profit."

Amanda got to see this firsthand. She kicked off her heels and joined the ranks in jeans and a T-shirt to raid a puppy mill in the South. Eighty-eight dogs were saved in an all-day raid on a breeding operation. "These animals are in some of the worst conditions we've seen," said Kim Alboum, Director of the Humane Society of North Carolina. "They're in their feces. They have nails growing into their paw pads, ear infections, and eye infections." And Amanda saw that the breeder dogs were matted, mangy, on top of each other with no room to move about and often kept in these conditions to breed and breed for their whole lives.

Amanda winced. "It's heartbreaking," she said. "They're in crates on top of each other and it is horrible to see them! I had to remind myself that these are getting rescued, and we did rescue all of them!"

In that moment, she saw the start in life that Finnegan got. Who knew? So she started Friends of Finn to work with the Humane Society to raise money and to tell the world about these deplorable conditions.

"Finnegan is almost four years old," said Amanda. "I bought him at a pet store and they told me he was from a breeder, but then I found out he was from a puppy mill of almost nine hundred dogs and it was horrible."

Our start in life informs our future. Where we came from has a big impact on our lives. Dogs and people all need nourishment, caring, and clean conditions for their start.

"My best advice," Amanda said, "is to adopt from a shelter rather than buying from a pet store. Animal shelters have many pure-bred and mixed-breed lovable dogs who are looking for a forever home."

Amanda gushes about her puppy love, and how that love inspired her compassion and hope for less fortunate animals. Amanda's gifts at the start of her life have given gifts and more gifts to other creatures, and she plans to bring more awareness and financial support to care for dogs and animals through the works of the Humane Society and Friends of Finn.

Spinning Wheels Got to Go Round

Caryn Rosenthal

When I rescued a little dachshund/spaniel mix from North Shore Animal League in New York City, I did not imagine that his six pounds of puppy love eventually would show me what courage meant. I named him Jax, but around my Upper West Side neighborhood, his name quickly became "John Gotti" because of his "big shot" attitude even though he was small.

For the first year and a half, he was a happy dog with no cares in the world. We had a great life living it up in the Big Apple or playing on the beach in Jacksonville, Florida, where I vacation during the winter months. Then Jax developed a disc problem that affected his back legs. The vet said it may have been caused by a larger dog falling on him when he was in the shelter. As time went on, it became more and more difficult for Jax to walk. I tried carrying him, but he wanted no part of this. He started sulking around the house and became a different dog. He lost his appetite and seemed to lose his will to live. I had no idea what to do and called the vet.

The vet suggested spinal surgery as the only solution to repair his back legs and regain his happy personality. I was hopeful this would fix the problem so Jax could regain his active lifestyle. The vet told me not to expect too much the first month. He said if the surgery was successful, Jax would begin to show improvement during the second month. Unfortunately, after a three-month recovery period, he still could not use his hindquarters. I felt as if I had lost my best friend. He slept most of the day because it took so much effort for him to move. Even in his sleep, I could see him wince from pain. He became more miserable and was completely immobile. I felt hopeless and helpless.

One day as I was telling a friend about Jax's condition, she suggested a solution: "Call Doggon' Wheels. This organization can fit Jax with something to help him get around again," she said.

The next morning, I got in touch with them. They not only took Jax's measurements to fit him with a mobility device, they also gave me hope that my dog could enjoy life again. This wonderful organization only took a week to make and send an "all-terrain vehicle" customized for Jax.

I knew it was going to take time, but I believed Jax could learn to maneuver his new device and regain some mobility. In the beginning, I was able to control the amount of weight he placed on his rear legs. It only took a few days of practice for him to learn how to "go potty" on the newspaper in the kitchen while on wheels.

I quickly learned Jax was no quitter. With each failure, I could see the determination growing in his eyes as if they said, "I am not giving up. I will do this!" He showed so much heart and courage. I gave him all the help and time he needed. We worked together as a finely tuned team. I gradually adjusted the weight until he was able to support himself completely. It was not easy for him to adapt, but gradually, he got more comfortable using his wheels on the hardwood floor of my apartment.

After a week of practicing indoors, I decided it was time to do a test-drive outdoors. I was nervous as I carried Jax outside, but tried not to show it. As I gingerly set him down on the sidewalk, he looked up at me. Then he looked to the right and left, remembering the route we used to walk. I took a step and Jax followed confidently. The next step we did together. Soon we were walking at our normal pace. My neighbors, who had not seen him since before his operation, were astounded at how well he was doing. They remembered how difficult it had been for him to walk as his degenerative disc worsened.

Soon they began calling him "Fearless Jax" because he was not afraid to try anything. On our walks in Central Park, Jax began chasing horses on the bridal paths as if it was something he had always done. When we visited the gorgeous Conservatory Garden, he would find lots of places to sniff under and around the beautiful plants. We began running four miles a day, rain or shine. He chased anything that even slightly resembled a ball, with his wheels spinning fast in order to keep up with his front legs.

We took long hikes on rough-winding trails up and down steep hills in upstate New York. I would let Jax off leash and he would roll through the brambles chasing rabbits and squirrels. When he got tangled up in the brush, he waited patiently as I cleared the wheels. As soon as I said, "Go, Jax," he would be off chasing something else.

His personality changed from being a cute little dog to one with the personality of a four-legged, two-hundred-pound Rottweiler. He was in charge once again.

The more places we visited, the more people began to approach me to find out more about Jax. After all, it is not every day you see a tiny dog on wheels. When they heard his story, they were amazed at how well he was able to manage. Some people even recorded him rolling along in the park and uploaded their videos to YouTube. His celebrity began to spread like wildfire. At first, I received calls from the local media who wanted to write about him in their newspapers.

One day I received a call for an interview from PEOPLEPets.com. The following week, the New York *Daily News* sent a reporter and photographer for an article about Jax's rehabilitation. Next, he appeared on MSNBC. But the biggest thrill was when I received a call from NBC-TV that Jane Hanson wanted Jax to appear on *New York Live*. She was astounded at the ability Jax showed as he wheeled around the studio. A cameraman even commented that he was "hell on wheels" as he skillfully maneuvered around the equipment and props. Jax was even featured in a couple of short films, yet he took his new celebrity status in stride.

Jax has become an ambassador of courage that spreads the word about how to never give up, no matter how much life throws at you. He has proven you cannot keep a good dog down for long.

Phoebe and Belle

The Courageous Ones

Basia Christ

During the spring of 1958, my parents abandoned me. I was twelve years old. My paternal grandparents ended up raising me, and they took me to the local pound to let me get a puppy. They thought it might help me through that tough time.

I found a beautiful puppy who I named Phoebe. She was part Doberman pinscher and part Manchester terrier. I had never had a dog, and she became my best friend and confidant.

While I was growing up on the near West Side of Chicago, my neighborhood changed drastically. It went from a safe place for kids to be out late at night to an area where gangs ruled the streets. My grandmother warned me not to walk Phoebe at night, but like any kid, I didn't listen. I thought my grandmother was overprotective, and I felt safe with Phoebe at my side. I was wrong.

One summer evening when I was sixteen, I snuck out to take Phoebe for a walk. As I walked past an alley, I was hit from behind. As I fell to the ground, I let go of the leash and lost consciousness.

When I awoke, my head hurt terribly and I was bleeding. Phoebe lay at my side. People surrounded me and asked if I was all right. According to a neighbor, a man had attacked me and Phoebe attacked him. Whatever he hit me with, he had hit Phoebe with, too.

I struggled to my feet and realized only my head was injured. I was thankful I was alive. When I grabbed Phoebe's leash, she couldn't stand up. It was then I noticed her bloody, broken leg and the large bump on her head. She had saved my life, but sustained terrible injuries defending me.

For the next four years, Phoebe suffered from spasms. The vet said it was because of the brain injury she received from my attacker. Every time she had one, I held her in my arms until the shaking stopped. One day, the spasms were extremely severe. Once again, I held her tightly in my arms. She looked at me so sadly and then took her last breath. I was still crying while holding her in my arms when my grandparents returned from the grocery store.

When I married and had three children, we acquired a variety of dogs and cats from various shelters. Only once did I purchase a dog from a pet store; my husband wanted a golden retriever, so my children got him a puppy named Nugget for a Father's Day gift one year.

Within three months, the vet diagnosed Nugget had hip dysplasia. When I called the pet store, I was told I had two options. I could bring Nugget back and get a replacement or keep her. When I said I would report them, they agreed to let us keep her, and would give us another retriever at a later date. A year later, we took them up on their offer and picked up another golden, which we named Cinnamon because of her red color. She looked more like a Labrador, but my children loved her, so I didn't complain.

Within a year, she developed a thyroid condition and grew to twice the normal size of a female retriever. She weighed 120 pounds and was not the most intelligent dog.

I vowed never to purchase any pet from a pet store again.

A year before my divorce, we had four dogs and three cats. That year and the first year of being single, all the animals had to be put down for various illnesses. It broke my heart and I knew I did not ever want to go through putting an animal down again.

In 2001, two years after my divorce, my employer relocated me to Orange

County, California. My middle daughter, Elke, came with me, and we decided to start new lives.

She became a vet tech at an animal hospital and one day brought home Emma, a pit bull/boxer mix that someone brought into the hospital because she was injured. She was obviously homeless and a bag of bones with mange and eye infections. I took one look at my daughter and asked, "Why did you do this without asking me?"

She said, "I promise to take care of her, Mom, she will be my dog, you won't have to do a thing."

Within a day, I loved Emma as much as Elke did.

I did warn her not to bring home any more animals like she did when she was young. She promised and the three of us adjusted to our new lives.

A year later, Elke called to say a breeder had brought in eleven puppies and asked the doctor to put them down because the breeder didn't like the looks of them. "Elke, no," I said without letting her finish.

"But, Mom, one is the blue color, like your friend Shari's Weimaraner," she countered.

"Absolutely not. Do not bring another dog home. Please," I ended the debate. Or thought I did.

That evening, Elke presented me with a five-week-old terrier puppy. She was blue, beautiful, and had a little white star on her chest. I fell in love and so did Emma. I named her Blue Belle because her eyes were turquoise blue.

Emma thought she was Belle's mom and let Belle cuddle up next to her when they slept. When Shari came to see my new puppy, she took one look at her and said, "Do you know Belle's a pit bull?"

I disagreed. Elke knew I would never adopt a pit bull. I was convinced they were vicious animals and I was afraid of them although I had never known one. It was their reputation.

By the time Elke finally admitted that, yes, Belle was an American Staffordshire (aka pit bull), I could not part with this beautiful dog.

She is the best dog, just as Phoebe was, and so incredibly smart and sensitive. She loves children and people. She even lets little dogs bite her without retaliation.

Once when we were at a dog park, a full-grown German shepherd ran at me snarling and teeth bared. Four-month-old Belle stood between me and the dog, letting the other dog know not to take one step closer. When the owner finally rushed over, he told me to get my pit bull out of the park. I never went back.

Every time I come home, Belle greets me with lots of jumping and running around me like a top. The only time she didn't was on November 4, 2010, when I returned home from the hospital after donating my kidney to a stranger.

As I walked through the door with my friend Shari helping me, Belle ran to me and instantly stopped. She knew something was different. She then slowly walked over and licked my hand. For the next week, she wouldn't sleep with me as she usually did. Instead, she lay on the floor next to my bed.

A week later, I woke up with her lying next to me. She knew I was well on the road to recovery.

Two rescues and my protectors, Phoebe and Blue Belle, have left an imprint on my heart that will never go away. I owe my life to them.

The Buzz on Biggie

Coppy Holzman

My daughter, Logan, a junior high school student at the time, was out shopping at a popular mall on the Post Road in Westport, Connecticut. When she approached her favorite clothing store, Logan noticed an ASPCA mobile van parked outside. She didn't pay much attention to it. However, on her way out, she had to go past the back of the van.

The van door was slightly open. She heard a small bark coming from one of the crates. When she looked closer, a blond, shaggy, extremely skinny dog came to the front and began wagging its tail excitedly. She was drawn to it and made eye contact.

As the woman from the ASPCA began packing up to leave, Logan asked what kind of dog it was.

"It's a Labrador/terrier mix. Why, are you interested in adopting him?" the woman asked.

"No, I was just wondering what was going to happen to the dog since it hadn't been adopted," Logan said. After hearing what would probably happen to him she immediately called and told me about the dog.

I tried reasoning with her. After all, we already had Camby, a cairn terrier who wasn't fond of other dogs. "Logan, you know how Camby is. I wouldn't want to upset our home by bringing a stray into it."

"But, Dad, pulllllleeeease, just come to see him. The ASPCA woman said this wasn't the first time she tried to get him adopted. And because no one wanted him today, his chances of getting adopted are almost impossible. He'll probably end up in a crate all alone for the rest of his life with no one to love him," Logan pleaded.

Reluctantly, I drove down to speak with the woman. As she opened the back of the van, Logan rushed to the crate and the dog's tail started wagging incessantly.

As Logan petted the dog, the woman told me how the dog came into her possession: "Biggie was found roaming the streets in North Carolina. A woman called the Humane Society when he was eating out of her garbage can. He didn't have any identification or collar, so she thought the best thing was to have him picked up. He was filthy and malnourished, full of fleas, and had a bad case of mange. He was shipped to Connecticut because our state doesn't put the animals to sleep. We cleaned him up the best we could, but we haven't been successful in finding him a home. Most people want a puppy so he's been with us for a while."

I looked at this straggly dog. My mind told me I was asking for trouble if I took the dog home, but as I looked into its eyes, "no" simply was no longer an option. My heart made the decision for me.

"Okay, Logan, but you have to promise that if Camby doesn't accept this dog, we'll have to return it."

"I promise, Dad, and I'll take care of him, too. You won't have to do a thing!"

Logan kept her word. As soon as we got home, she ran ahead and put Camby on the leash and brought her outside to introduce them, which is what the woman from the ASPCA had suggested.

Biggie was immediately submissive and lay on his back as Camby, obviously the alpha dog, sauntered over to give him a quick once-over. "So far, so good, Dad," Logan said happily.

Yes, I was surprised at Biggie's reaction to Camby. Instead of standing toe-to-toe with her, he did everything he could to let Camby know he was no threat,

---

---

even though he was three times the little dog's size. I guess he learned that to survive on the streets, you had to learn to get along quickly. However, Camby's reaction was even more startling. As we led the two dogs into our home, Camby took the lead and never looked back.

We named him "Biggie Smalls" after the late rapper and his hip-hop star. Unfortunately, he wasn't house-trained, so the first few weeks were hard, but Logan kept her promise and cleaned up after the dog. She brushed his long blondish hair more than she brushed her own. She even trained him to do some tricks. Within a few months, she had him sitting up, playing dead, and eventually getting the newspaper without tearing it to pieces.

Biggie adjusted quickly to "the good life." He now lived in a beautiful home on the Long Island Sound near the water. He was safe, had a warm home, and his own doggy door so he could go outside whenever he wanted. He made a game out of chasing the geese out of our yard by barking at them. Camby sat and watched, but once in a while, even she would let out a little bark, too. I think what Biggie enjoyed the most, though, was the loving family who adopted him.

Biggie soon began greeting visitors to our home in the driveway and taking their hands gently to escort them into the foyer. Our neighbors named Biggie "Mr. Sociable" because his tail is constantly wagging and he is always ready to play fetch.

This was Biggie's life for six years until we moved to Manhattan and he had to adjust to the elite business world. Although we reside in a chic loft downtown, Biggie and I walk up Fifth Avenue each morning to my midtown Charitybuzz office.

Biggie rushes to greet every vendor, doorman, and construction worker who knows him by name. Some even have treats for him, which he thoroughly enjoys. Visitors to my office also enjoy Biggie's presence, as he sits on his fluffy bed near our conference table. When he gets bored, he'll roam the halls and look for attention from my staff in their offices.

We took Biggie off the streets, but some habits die hard. Occasionally, I'll find

Biggie rummaging through a garbage can, looking for a discarded sandwich or candy wrapper. When I catch him, all I have to do is look at him harshly, and he immediately drops whatever treasure he found like a hot potato.

Looking back at old pictures from when Biggie came to live with us so many years ago, I have to laugh. Back then his long hair was constantly matted. It took many hours to brush him, but Logan never complained. Now Biggie sports a spiky Mohawk, "New York style." He's come a long way from eating garbage on the streets of North Carolina to taking a big bite out of the Big Apple.

27 Chance

The Chance of a Lifetime

Dan Shaw

I had mixed feelings during our Christmas holidays in 2008. Yes, spending time with family members and friends was wonderful, but I was still grieving for my beloved dog, Lisa, who had died from kidney failure a few months earlier. The holidays just weren't the same without Lisa ripping the wrapping paper and pushing around the empty boxes to see if I had missed something. She was always fun to watch during meals as she tried to sneak under the table quietly to get a morsel from someone's hand or find a speck of food that had fallen to the floor.

Even though many people believe this time of the year is special, a time when miracles can happen, I never really thought it could happen to me. Yet on the morning of December 26, little did I know my miracle was about to begin with a frantic phone call from a dear friend.

I was relaxing with my partner, enjoying the afterglow of Christmas when I received that call from Christine Madruga, founder of The Pet Rescue Center in Coachella, California. When I answered, I didn't even have time to say hello before she starting speaking quickly.

"Hi," she said. "I just happened to be at the pound when a staff member rushed in with a tiny white cockapoo/Maltese puppy that was run over by a car and left for dead in a remote area outside of Palm Springs. She's in a lot of pain and terrified. The vet says she's in bad shape. I waited to find out the extent of the stray's injuries before calling. She has five pelvic fractures, a hip fracture, and extensive nerve and tissue damage to one of her back legs. The vet said she'll never be able to use it again. I asked what was going to happen to her, and was told they were going to put the puppy down because the surgery will cost so much."

I started to say something, but she cut me off by assuring me she told the vet her nonprofit would cover the cost, but she wanted to ask me something important. She said, "I've named her Lois. I remembered you telling me about how sad you've been since Lisa died. I thought you might be interested in giving this puppy a second chance to live."

I asked Christine to hold on while I explained what was happening to my partner. Without hesitation, he yelled into the phone, "When can we see her?"

Christine asked me to hold on while she spoke to the vet. It seemed like hours before I heard her say, "The vet said the puppy would need at least a day of rest after the surgery. He said tomorrow would be the soonest you could visit."

Bright and early the next morning, we drove to the vet's office to get our first glimpse of the puppy. When we arrived, the vet greeted us in the foyer. He said, "The puppy came through the surgery like a champ. We did the best we could, but only time will tell how much she can recover any use of that leg." He then took us to the crate where the little dog was recuperating from the surgery. She looked so small and helpless in the large crate. It was hard to imagine someone hitting a puppy and leaving it on the road without trying to help.

We knelt down next to the crate where the puppy's head was resting comfortably on a blanket. I put my finger outside the bar trying not to startle her. Her eyes were open, but obviously she was still groggy. She lifted her head as best she could, leaned forward, and slowly licked my extended finger. Even though she was still in pain, she knew we were there for her. Then she laid her head down and closed her eyes.

With tears in our eyes, we stood up. As we looked down at the sleeping ball of white fur, we knew this puppy was special. I called Christine immediately and told her I wanted to adopt her. In fact, when I called I actually said, "The puppy is coming home with us when she's well."

Because my mother's name was Lois, I wanted to give this puppy a name of her own. I knew immediately that I would name her Chance. It fit her perfectly. I was giving the puppy a second chance, but she was also giving me a chance to love another dog.

For the next two weeks, I visited Chance almost daily at the animal hospital while she regained her strength and appetite. However, within a few days after bringing her home, I noticed her leg was not healing properly. She struggled to get her balance when trying to stand up. When she tried to walk, she dragged her back leg or tripped over it when she was tired.

The following week, the vet recommended amputating the leg in order to improve the puppy's mobility. After another surgery, Chance was quickly able to adapt to life with three legs and slowly got her puppy energy into high gear.

Friends say I've spoiled her, but how can you spoil a puppy that had such a rocky start to life? I'm just trying to make up for the months she was homeless and in pain.

Chance is an important part of our lives now. This little puppy proudly wears her bejeweled collar and when it's cold, she picks from a variety of colorful sweaters by standing on the one she wants. When we're outside, her favorite spot is on the front of my bicycle in the blue canvas bag with the soft white lining. With the wind in my hair and her ears, we attract a lot of attention from passersby as we cross the bridge in the park. People stop me so they can pet her and give her treats. Some even say she actually looks likes she smiling.

I believe our favorite time together is when Chance accompanies me to horse shows when I compete. She is my biggest supporter as I make the jumps and maneuver Felix my horse, through the gates. Even though I love to hear the crowd applaud, the real music to my ears is Chance's loud barking. She is the love of my life!

The Next One Will Find You

Loretta Mosher

One evening during a rainy week in October, my young daughter, Santana, and I decided to get out of the house and visit Ann and Lawry, good friends who lived at the beach. I called to let them know when we were close. When Ann answered, she warned me she had a full house.

I asked her to explain and she said, "A few days ago, Lawry spotted three strays, two poodle-mix puppies and a large poodle, that were running as a pack in a thunderstorm on the train tracks near his work in an industrial area. He could tell they were homeless because they had no collars, were filthy, and extremely emaciated. He immediately stopped his car. As he approached, Lawry saw how terrified they were. When he heard the train whistle, he knew the train was near. He had to act fast. His first impulse was to run after them."

Ann explained how Lawry was able to catch the puppies fairly quickly and put them into the backseat of his car. However, the poodle was faster than the lightning flashing all around them in the sky. The more he called and ran after the dog, the more the dog tried to escape. Lawry decided on a different approach. He stood still, kneeled down, and tried to coax the dog to him with a reassuring voice.

Lawry could hear the train was fast approaching. When the poodle saw the metal beast, it froze on the tracks. Lawry tried to stay calm, knowing he had only a short time to save the dog. He held out his hand and spoke quietly, almost in a whisper, while ignoring the train. The dog responded immediately, perhaps instinctively realizing that he had nothing to fear from this stranger. As soon as he let Lawry gently pick him up, Lawry ran to his car and put the large dog in the backseat with the puppies.

Ann continued, "After putting the poodle with the puppies, Lawry turned around and saw the train cross the spot where he and the dog had been only moments earlier. He had to take a deep breath to calm himself before starting the car. By that time, all three dogs were jumping excitedly all over him, vying for his attention. They didn't realize the danger they just escaped!"

When we arrived, Ann and Lawry greeted us at the door followed closely behind by three bundles of fluffy energy—with tails wagging and bellies full.

My eyes immediately went to the male puppy. I knew instantly Santana and I were not going to leave without him. Weeks earlier, our sixteen-year-old kitty had passed away and we were still grieving our loss. As I looked into the puppy's blue eyes, I remembered what the vet had told me on that terrible day, "The next one will find you!"

And find us he did!

My daughter immediately scooped the puppy into her arms and asked our friends tearfully if we could take him home. I laughed because she had read my mind.

Ann and Lawry celebrated our split decision with a toast of hot tea and homemade chocolate chip cookies. As we said good-bye, I wondered how my husband was going to react when he saw Santana carrying this warm ball of fur into our home.

I needn't have worried. He looked at the puppy's soulful face, took him gently from Santana's arms, and the puppy immediately started licking his cheeks. Within a few hours, they were rolling around the floor like two young ruffians.

We all suggested names, but decided on Santana's choice of "Mixer" because we could already tell he was going to mix himself right into our hearts, like sugar into a cake batter.

And did he ever!

I don't know if Mixer remembers his life before coming to us when he was running wild around on the train tracks with his little sister and the large poodle. When they were starving, cold, and wet. Without any human companionship or love. Lives that easily could have ended without anyone knowing or caring they had lived.

I do know, however, that Mixer understands he is safe and loved. His huge toy box is filled with colorful Frisbees, balls, and tugs with which to play. His meals are nutritious with tasty treats in-between. His soft bed is always clean, fluffed, and warm. His brown doggy blanket with white paw prints is tucked neatly at the end of the couch in "his place."

Mixer now is an important part of our family and goes everywhere with us. He gets nonstop attention and boundless love. When we're walking Mixer, he eagerly greets others with a wagging tail and endless energy that instantly makes people reach down and pet him. And he never gets tired of the attention.

One evening I looked around at our family outside in our yard. My husband and daughter were playing fetch with Mixer, his ears flapping wildly as he jumped high for the wooden stick, running back and forth tirelessly between them, and handing over the gooey prize in the hopes of another toss his way. I remembered how we felt when our kitty died and the hole it left in our hearts. I remembered my call to Ann on a whim to ask if Santana and I could come over for a visit that rainy evening, just days after Lawry's heroic efforts to save the lives of three strays at the risk of his own. I wondered which one of us benefited more that day when Santana carried Mixer into our hearts?

Was it my husband, who is greeted by Mixer, "his boy," with a big, wet slurp to the face after a long day at the office? Was it me, who knows when my husband is away on a business trip, Mixer will keep a watchful eye out the windows and lets me know immediately if a stranger is close? Was it Santana, who grooms and feeds Mixer so lovingly and doesn't even mind cleaning up after him? Was it Mixer, who found a family who loves him without question, even when he tramples muddy paws on a freshly washed floor or tips over the garbage can spilling trash everywhere? I can honestly say I don't wonder anymore. Each one of our lives is better!

Mixer gets to play with his sister and the poodle and their new families, too. Three families—and three precious creatures of God—whose lives were changed one rainy evening in October because someone cared, stopped, and saved them.

I thank God for people like Lawry. And every night I thank God for bringing Mixer to us and making our family whole again.

Living Life to the Max

Rene Dell'Acqua

My husband, Joe, and I already had rescued Coco, a Labrador, and two Shih Tzus named Isabella and Chloe from an animal shelter in Indio, California. We also adopted a stray cat that was wandering around our neighborhood. We certainly had no plans of adding any more animals to our family.

That was until a year later when my husband, my seven-year-old son, Joey, and I attended the Le Chien fashion show, which is a fund-raiser for the Humane Society of the Desert presented by *Palm Springs Life* magazine during Fashion Week in Palm Springs, California. We were sitting in the front row, and out on the runway came this huge black-and-brown Rottweiler. He walked with a limp and looked very sad. My heart melted. Joey tugged on my arm and whispered in my ear, "Mom, look!" I told him I was sure the dog belonged to someone, but Joey showed me the program that said he was up for adoption. Joe and I looked at each other. I immediately started shaking my head, "no," but my heart was telling me "yes."

We drove home and all the while Joe told Joey we were going to adopt the dog. I kept reminding them of the full house we had waiting for us at home, but it didn't seem to sink in. They finally got me to agree to go and see the dog; however, both of them knew I would give in.

The next day, Joe; Joey; my other son, Courtland; daughter, Aubrey; and I drove to the shelter and spoke to the Humane Society of the Desert's president, Malinda Bustos, who told us how she had rescued Jambawaya from a county shelter that euthanizes dogs because of space issues.

"I had gotten a call that they had an older Rottweiler that no one wanted and his time was up. I immediately drove there and took him under my wing. He was about forty pounds overweight and suffered from entropion, a condition where the eyelids turn in and the eyelashes irritate the cornea. Once we got Jamba down to a healthy weight, we were able to arrange the necessary surgery to correct the condition. Then we hired a trainer to work with him on obedience and house-training. Jamba has been with us for about eight months," Malinda said. "I thought showcasing him in the fashion show might make someone want to adopt him," she added, smiling at us.

She brought Jamba out to meet our family. He walked right over to me and started licking my hands and face. I wondered if Joe and Joey somehow told him I was the one he had to convince. As our children sat on the floor, Jamba calmly went to each of them and licked their hands and face as well. I looked at Joe as I said to Malinda, "We want to adopt him." We filled out the paperwork and came to pick up Jamba the next day.

Joey held the leash and led Jamba, who was bigger than him, to the car. On the drive home, we took turns trying to find the perfect name for our newest family member. We finally came up with the name, Massamiliano, Max for short. He looked nervously out the back window as if to say, "Where am I going now?"

By the time we reached our driveway, Max was already responding to his new name. When we brought him inside, the other dogs rushed over to make his acquaintance in their usual manner of sniffing. Max was cautious at first; however, within minutes, the other dogs made him feel welcome by rolling on their backs. Joe and I looked at each other. We knew we had made the right decision.

Since I had been taking the three dogs to work with me where they stay in a private office next to my dental practice, Joe decided to take Max to work with him in Orange County. However, the next morning I noticed a small growth on Max's side and took him to see the vet.

The vet was able to remove the lump, but told me that Max had problems with his anterior cruciate ligaments. After hearing that, I told Joe, "I can't bear to be away from Max. He's my baby." Now all four dogs pile into my little Fiat and come to work with me every day.

It took a while for Max to realize he was going to live with us. He wasn't as playful as the other dogs and never touched the toys. We purposely spent more time walking Max to build the strength in his back legs. He finally began to respond. He began to play with the other dogs and became more relaxed. He even jumps into our swimming pool and swims . . . like a water buffalo.

Max makes the rounds at night, first sleeping with Courtland, then Aubrey, but always settles down for the night by crawling into Joey's bed. When I see Max and Joey curled up in bed together, my heart melts.

We continue to see Max improve daily. He is becoming more mobile and it has given me so much happiness to see him play with the other dogs, too. Two weeks ago, Max started playing with toys. When a friend, who is a psychologist, told me that when your pet starts playing with toys it means it has healed from whatever sadness it was suffering, I cried.

We know most people want puppies, but when we rescued Max, even with his special needs, we knew he was going to be our companion and friend for life.

Adopting pets has changed my perspective about life. I had never rescued an animal before last summer when I saw pictures of Coco, Isabella, and Chloe on a Facebook page about dogs that needed to be rescued. All three opened my heart and mind to the idea of pet rescuing.

Our dogs are such special animals. They each have such different histories and each needed time to heal. We gave these dogs a home, but they have given us so much more joy than I could ever imagine.

30 Rootsie Tootsie, Nicole, Sparky, and Kissy

Four Plus One Equals Fun

Ruta Lee

Ruta Lee is a Canadian actress and dancer with an impressive history on stage and television. She was a frequent guest on a number of game shows such as *The Hollywood Squares* and *What's My Line?*, and even cohosted a game show with Alex Trebek called *High Rollers*.

The public Ruta loves being in the spotlight; however, the private Ruta is a wonderfully compassionate and philanthropic woman.

Years ago, she rescued a parrot named Samy. Life was quiet and good—except for an occasional squawk.

When a close friend asked Ruta and her husband, Webster "Webb" Lowe, to attend a charity auction for the benefit of homeless dogs hosted by The Share Group, they agreed.

One of the dogs being put up for adoption was a gorgeous poodle named Rootsie Tootsie donated by Cesar Millan, the Dog Whisperer. Bidding was fast and fierce. By the time the auctioneer called for any more bids, and there were none, Ruta was in disbelief that her friend had just paid $20,000 for the dog. "It's for charity," was her answer to Ruta's question of, "What were you thinking?"

Shortly after her friend took the dog home, the woman's husband and her housekeeper died. "When she asked if I wanted Rootsie Tootsie because she could not deal with the dog, I accepted," Ruta said.

A few months later, Ruta attended another charity event put on by The Thalians, which raises money for the maintenance of the Thalians Mental Health Center at Cedars-Sinai Medical Center.

Ruta hadn't planned on bringing another dog home, but then a big ball of white fluff walked down the "dogway." Ruta could not resist. She raised her number and hoped no one else would bid. No one did. "I think the reason there were no other bids was because no one knew exactly what kind of dog it was," Ruta offered.

After the auction, the first stop was to Rootsie Tootsie's groomer. When the groomer saw the big white ball of fluff, she asked what exactly Ruta wanted her to do. "I have no idea. Just try to make her look like something," was Ruta's answer.

The groomer called her three hours later and said the dog was ready. When Ruta arrived, there was only one dog in the shop, a beautiful poodle, so Ruta asked where her dog was.

"This IS your dog," the groomer answered.

Ruta was stunned. She could not believe this elegant-looking dog was the same dog.

As they walked to her car, people asked Ruta from what breeder she had gotten such a beautiful poodle. She said, "From the pound. There are always plenty to choose from." And she kept walking. Ruta decided to name her Nicole.

Rootsie Tootsie and Nicole were quite the pair. They soon became best friends.

Ruta and Webb heard about a little Yorkie named Sparky at a local shelter, whose time was almost up. She called and they told her they would hold the dog for her if she could get there that very afternoon.

Ruta drove right over. "When I asked why this dog had not been adopted, the manager hesitated for a moment and said, 'He has been adopted, twice, but returned each time.'"

As Ruta left holding Sparky, she had a little heart-to-heart with him. By the time she arrived home, her husband looked at the little dog she was holding and just smiled.

When Rootsie Tootsie and Nicole ran over to Sparky to check him out, the dog did the strangest thing. He began running in circles. The two dogs stopped in their tracks. Ruta lifted the dog and tried to calm him.

When he seemed to have settled down, Ruta again put him on the grass. He began running in circles again, even faster than the first time. "I figured it out quickly. When Sparky is frightened, he just runs in circles," Ruta said.

After a few weeks, the circles made in the grass were fewer and fewer as the three dogs became friends.

Ruta never liked odd numbers. So off to the shelter she went one more time to even out her pack. This time she brought home Kissy. "She is the sweet one that loves to be held. She is perfectly happy to watch the other three's doggy antics from the comfort of my lap," Ruta said.

However, Kissy joins in the play when Samy is let out of his cage. The parrot becomes the drum major and parades all four dogs around the pool. And sometimes Ruta joins in.

Rescuing four dogs and one bird has not stopped Ruta from continuing her support of homeless animals. She is a member of Actors & Other Animals, a long-standing Los Angeles animal welfare organization, and she is very active with The Thalians charity group.

At the last "Broadway World Event," a Best in Show competition and luncheon, Ruta commented, "It is so much fun to spend the afternoon with two-legged friends who are almost as nice as our four-legged ones."

31 Buddy

Riding Shotgun

Lisa Sickler Watts

It had been a hectic morning. I got up late and had to rush to get my boys off to school on time. I was running late for my doctor's appointment, but was happy traffic was moving at a good pace on the six-lane freeway. Suddenly, I heard tires squealing, but couldn't see what was happening ahead. Something was causing cars to swerve out of their lanes.

Then a huge golden Lab ran in front of my car. I quickly changed lanes to avoid hitting it. The car next to me ran off onto the shoulder to avoid an accident. I said a silent prayer the dog would reach the safety of the field next to the highway as I watched it running wildly in my rearview mirror.

While waiting for the doctor, all I could think about was the frightened dog running for its life. I wondered if it was all right.

Two hours later, I was on my way home on the freeway and was astounded when, once again, I heard brakes squealing and watched traffic come to a complete stop. I couldn't believe my eyes. There was the golden Lab, still disoriented and running back and forth across the freeway. Several people got out of their cars to chase it.

I could tell it was frightened and agitated. The fur on its back was raised; its eyes wide open. It was understandable since people were trying to corner it. The dog didn't know they were trying to save it.

Without thinking, I jumped out of my car, opened the rear door, and yelled, "Come on, Buddy! Get in the car! Let's go bye-bye!"

Everyone stopped chasing the dog. The dog stopped running. A moment later, it ran to me, panting as it jumped into my car. I slammed the door shut as a would-be rescuer shouted, "Is that your dog?"

For a moment I wondered what possessed me to let this wild creature into my car. He was whining and shaking. What if it had rabies? What if it attacked me when I got back into my car?

I answered, "No, it's not mine. I don't know what I was thinking. It happened so fast. I just wanted to get the dog off the freeway safely!"

Everyone exchanged phone numbers and took pictures of the dog, so we could make posters. I was truly moved by their concern for this stray.

I looked in the backseat. By this time the dog had laid down, obviously exhausted from its morning of literally running for its life. It was matted and dirty. It didn't have any identification.

I got in the car and sat there for a moment, wondering what to do next. Should I take it to the pound? Should I take it to a vet? Should I take it home? Luckily, I didn't have to decide. The dog decided for me when it sat up and put a dirty paw on my shoulder. When I turned around, it licked my face. When I smiled, it immediately jumped into the front seat next to me.

I rubbed its back as I drove home. It sat upright and watched traffic whiz by that only a few moments earlier could have killed him. As I pulled into my garage and opened the door, Buddy jumped across my lap as if he had done it many times before, as if he knew this was his new home. I wondered what my sons would think when they got home from school and saw this matted, dirty dog.

When they opened the door, the dog ran to greet them. Marcus, my thirteen-year-old, yelled excitedly, "Where did you get him?" Eight-year-old, Robbie, already had his arms wrapped around the dog's neck. Thomas, eleven, ran to get a ball from his room so they could play catch.

In stereo, they asked, "Can we keep him?" I explained what happened. They immediately began calling him "Buddy" so no discussion was necessary to name him.

First order of business was to wash and groom him. My oldest started the bath, while the rest of us gathered towels and shampoo. Robbie offered his hairbrush until we could get Buddy one of his own.

As Marcus began the tough job of getting the knots out of Buddy's fur, I called the local pound and gave them a description of Buddy. Next, we took his picture and made posters. Thomas and Robbie plastered them around the neighborhood. Secretly, I wished no one would claim Buddy.

The next day I got an appointment with a vet who said Buddy obviously had been on the street for a long time. He was undernourished and had fleas. After giving Buddy the proper shots and medication, the vet explained how, since times were hard, many people drop their animals in upscale neighborhoods hoping they will get adopted.

I called the pound manager every day to ask if anyone reported a golden Lab missing. For two weeks, no one responded to the posters. I also called the other drivers to see if they had any luck. By the third week, the pound manager said if no one claimed the dog by now, no one probably would.

That same evening, I made a special meal for Buddy, officially welcoming him into our family. The boys had pooled their allowances and presented Buddy with a plush brown bed, chew toys, a yellow Frisbee, a collar with his name engraved on a shiny tag, and lots of hugs! My contribution was a large crate with a wooden sign with BUDDY carved in large letters. It was official. We had a new family member.

Buddy became an instant hit in our neighborhood, too. The neighbors refer to me as the "Lady with the Golden Dog!" Buddy brought my sons closer as they happily shared the necessary chores of feeding, bathing, grooming, and cleaning up after Buddy. While doing their homework, they spread their books on the floor so Buddy could lie next to them. Buddy attended all their baseball games, too. He

was their loudest cheerleader as everyone in the stands came to know his unique bark.

It's been eight years now, but I can still see those school mornings, when Buddy and the boys would race to the car to claim shotgun. No matter who got to the seat first, Buddy would sit on him until he gave up. Buddy claimed shotgun all those years ago, and it's still his rightful place today. And, after all this time, what Buddy loves best is to jump into the car and "go bye-bye."

Cherie, Tilly, Jacqueline, Toots, and Lillian

The Right Place at the Right Time

Kaye Ballard

Kaye Ballard knew by the ripe old age of five years old that she wanted to be a performer—and not just any type of performer, she wanted to sing. She wanted to dance. She wanted to make people laugh.

She began performing in burlesque and vaudeville even before she graduated from high school. She toured with the famous Spike Jones Orchestra as their vocalist and tuba player.

During her lifetime, she has been on the cover of *Life* magazine, played the Tooth Fairy on *Captain Kangaroo*, and had tea with Mother Teresa in the Bronx. She has appeared in numerous films, on the stage, and on television. "I got many breaks because I was in the right place at the right time," Kaye offered.

She has always been known as a performer with a big heart; however, her close friends know she has always had a big soft spot for dogs that need a good home.

Kaye purchased Jacqueline, a show-quality dog, for a lot of money. The dog was difficult to train and had a diva attitude to boot. She was such high maintenance, Kaye was happy there was just one of her.

Cherie came into Kaye's life quite by accident. Once while Kaye was getting her hair done, her hairdresser got a call from her next appointment who said she was not coming. Her ninety-year-old mother had become very ill and was being transferred to a hospice facility. The client was naturally upset, but when she said she had to find a home for her mother's dog immediately, the hairdresser suggested she bring the dog to her salon.

When the daughter showed up with this fluffy, little dog, Kaye fell in love. "I thought maybe the dog would occupy Jacqueline and keep her out of trouble. It didn't work out that way. Cherie was well-behaved, but her good behavior did not rub off on Jacqueline. The next time I had my hair done, my hairdresser told me the mother and daughter died within forty-eight hours of each other. It was meant for me to adopt Cherie," Kaye said.

About a year later, Kaye was having lunch in her favorite restaurant when a waitress carried in a little scruffy dog she had found wandering the streets of Palm Springs. She asked if anyone wanted it, and, without hesitation, Kaye stood up and said, "I'll take her."

She took the dog to her vet for a checkup. He said the dog was about nine years old and had been a stray for a while considering her condition. She was malnourished and covered with fleas. After the vet, Kaye immediately took the dog, which she named Tilly, to her favorite groomer, Ritzy Rover. "Tilly came out looking like 'The Best in Show,'" Kaye remarked. "I didn't realize how beautiful she was under all that dirty, matted fur."

Thankfully, Cherie and Tilly became great friends while Jacqueline continued her mischievous ways.

Not long after that, one of Kaye's acquaintances, who was extremely fanatical about his home, called Kaye and asked if she wanted another dog. Kaye felt lucky that Cherie and Tilly got along, but wondered what might happen if she brought another dog home.

When he explained that from the moment Toots stepped into his home, she constantly barked, Kaye decided she would not take the dog. Before she could say anything, he added that his remedy had been to keep her in a cage most of the day. Right after he said that, he added if Kaye did not take the dog, his next option was to drop the dog off at the shelter. Without giving it another thought, Kaye said she would come right away.

"Toots is such a gentle dog. All she ever wanted was some attention. Between Cherie, Tilly, Jacqueline, and I, Toots gets plenty now. And the best news is, she has stopped barking," Kaye added.

Then there were four. And Kaye loved every minute of their antics. By this time, Jacqueline was not getting into as much trouble. No, she still was not what one would call well-behaved, but she was making progress and slowly learning from the other dogs' good behavior.

About a year later, one of Kaye's close friends called to say a friend of hers had to move into an apartment that did not allow pets so she had to find homes for her two little dogs. Luckily, one friend was going to take one of the dogs to Paris. And Kaye took Lillian.

As Kaye introduced Lillian to her other dogs, they welcomed her with doggy kisses and sniffs. As they all took off running in a pack, Kaye had a sudden epiphany: "I had no intention of having five dogs, but it seemed as if I was destined to rescue these dogs. I guess I could sum it up by saying, just like during my career, I was in the right place at the right time."

33 Constantine

The Conqueror of Hearts

David Evans

One April Sunday, while I was holding an open house for clients whose home I was representing as their realtor, another realtor brought a client to see the home. She was quite excited, not just about showing the home, but also because she had found a large puppy at their previous stop just sitting on the doorstep. After speaking with the neighbors, she discovered the home had been vacant for a while. Evidently, the owners packed up everything except the puppy, who had to fend for itself. She couldn't leave it, so her immediate reaction was to take it with her.

"I have other homes to show my client today. Would you mind if I left the puppy here for a while?" she pleaded. Realizing what a predicament she was in, I agreed. She gave me her card and took mine, agreeing to call me when she was finished with her client. She said she would take the puppy to the local animal control shelter.

I agreed because the garage was empty, and my clients were animal-loving friends. I started to tell her they would see this little guy needed help, and that it was the right thing to do.

Before I even finished the sentence, the realtor went to her minivan and opened the back door. Out sprang a big floppy-eared puppy that might have been a retriever. My estimate was that he was about three months old because of how uncoordinated he was. I could tell he had been badly neglected. He was covered from head to toe with sharp thorns, but he was friendly. It was love at first sight.

He was quiet during the open house, which proved he was not a barker. When I opened the door to the garage, he ran to me as if I was his long-lost best friend. He rolled over onto his back and I rubbed his belly. I could tell by his perpetually wagging tail that he was very friendly. All these traits made the decision to take him home easier. I called the other realtor and told her not to worry about coming to get the puppy. I was going to take him home.

Now all I had to do was convince my wife, Carrie, why we needed to welcome this dog into our home. While driving home, I prepared a speech. I thought of every conceivable objection she might imagine and had a pat answer to counter it.

I made one stop at the pet store to buy puppy food; a large, soft doggy bed; a collar; and leash. And some pads just in case he wasn't house-trained. I felt I was prepared for any situation this puppy might present as I parked in our garage.

While waiting for Carrie to come home, I fed the puppy and he ate ravenously. I took him out into our front yard to see if he would know what to do. He immediately began to mark his territory on my wife's prize rose bushes. I quickly took him back into the house as I looked online and found a dog repellant for plants. That objection was covered. Still, I was happy I bought the pads, just in case.

When the neighborhood kids saw the puppy bounce out of the front door with me close behind, they were drawn to it, as kids usually are. By the time Carrie arrived home, she was greeted by the sight of a large puppy being chased by a group of children with me standing on the doorstep smiling, taking it all in.

She parked the car, got out, and looked at me with angry eyes that demanded to know, "What is this puppy doing here?" However, before she could get the words out, the puppy charged and jumped into her arms. She looked at me with surprise as a huge smile spread across her face. My rehearsed arguments weren't needed. She asked how I got the puppy. As I told her, the puppy ran around our legs in circles. We looked down and knew he was ours without question. We named him Constantine.

Over the next few days, we discovered Constantine was voraciously hungry and thirsty. We couldn't fill his bowls fast enough. He also was afraid of the dark and loud noises. As nighttime came, Constantine would howl, not bark, if he heard anything outside. He would then prowl the house, checking every window and door before he could relax and go to sleep again.

He was also afraid of the dark and loud noises. As nighttime came, Constantine would howl, not bark, if he heard anything outside. He would then prowl the house, checking every window and door before he could relax and go to sleep again.

However, the worst situation with which we had to deal was that Constantine was afraid of wearing a collar or being tied up. We imagined this might have happened because he was punished or abused when he was collared or tied up. We worked with him patiently for months until he learned to trust us. We never put a collar on him while he's at home. Now when we reach for the collar and leash, he knows we're all going for a walk, which he loves.

Since the neighborhood kids had already met Constantine, when they saw us walking toward them, they would run into their homes and get their parents to come out and meet the puppy, too. We met our neighbors with Constantine's help. If he sees new neighbors moving into our neighborhood, he will pull on his leash to welcome them before the moving vans are unloaded.

We also learned Constantine's attention span was minus ten. If he notices anything flying, he will chase it, from flies to butterflies to balls to airplanes. He loves to play catch and is proud of his enormous collection of tennis balls, some of which have been buried in our yard like treasure.

Because of our success with Constantine, we rescued another dog, Rudy, whose story is a different chapter in our lives.

Years later, we had a DNA test done on Constantine and were told he was part German shepherd, Akita, Doberman, and American Staffordshire terrier mix. He has all the positive traits of these noble breeds and is the smartest, most energetic, most curious, and most loving dog we ever owned. We initially didn't have a reason for naming him Constantine, but I realize it is the perfect name as he conquered our hearts and we surrendered completely.

The Underdog That Realized His Dream

David Evans

I was in a hurry to get home and anxious to get out of the questionable neighborhood, known for gang violence, through which the detour was taking me. It had been a long day and now it was going to take me even longer to get home.

It was getting dark. I couldn't imagine anything that would make me stop. Out of the corner of my eye, I saw a dark fleeting shadow and immediately turned my head in its direction.

A large, skinny dog was about to dart in front of my car. My foot slammed on the brakes. My car came to a screeching halt. So did the dog. For a moment, he looked like the proverbial "deer in the headlights." I could see he had no collar, was frightened, and in bad shape. Then he took off running to the other side of the street before I could react.

I got out of my car waving a half of a sandwich left over from lunch. That got his attention. He lunged at it. I was afraid he was going to take my hand along with the sandwich, so I dropped part of it in the street. It didn't seem to matter to him; he gulped it down without chewing. I still had a piece in my hand, so I opened the back door, threw it into the backseat, and the dog followed. After swallowing the rest of the sandwich, he turned around to realize there was no escape. He slid down onto the floor, cowered, and began shaking.

I remembered the day Constantine came into my life. This time I didn't think my wife, Carrie, would be such a pushover. Then again, I didn't think she'd question my bringing him home and rescuing him from his present state of living on the streets.

As I parked my car, I had no idea what I was going to say. As I opened the front door to our home with the dog following, I began speaking. "Before you say anything, Carrie, let me tell you what happened."

After finishing my story, I ended with, "And I'm just going to take him to the vet, get him fixed up, and drop him off at a shelter. Honest."

Constantine came into the room and quickly there was fur flying everywhere. Since both dogs came from the streets, Constantine fought to defend his territory. The other dog was just trying to stay alive.

Neither dog had a collar, so separating them was difficult. Trying to avoid their snapping jaws was our main priority; getting them apart was an important second. I told Carrie to lift Constantine's back legs at the same time I lifted the other dog's back legs. It worked. Both dogs stopped fighting.

Carrie took Constantine to another room and came back, arms crossed. All she said was, "Call the vet," and went to attend to our dog.

Thankfully, our vet, Dr. Ann Eliopoulos, was able to fit the dog into her schedule. She shook her head slowly as she opened the door to the treatment room. After an initial exam, she suggested leaving him overnight to do additional tests and X-rays. Because she does a lot of pro bono work for the local shelter, she said she would consider this visit as such.

The next morning, Dr. Ann called and said, "The dog did really well last night." She went on to say the dog was super sweet although he had had a hellish life. "His X-rays show profound past injury on his right back leg. It was never treated and is two inches shorter than the other legs. Other fractures have healed on their own as well. The dog will eventually need some surgery. I can tell by his toenails he's been living on the streets for a long time. He quite possibly was used as bait in dogfighting. He has scarring over fifty percent of his body coupled with severe hair loss and tremendous skin damage. He's got a great spirit considering what he's lived through. He's lucky to have found you. You saved his life."

I sat down wondering what to do. How could I just drop this poor dog off at a shelter knowing that even if he was in great condition, the chance that he might not get adopted was high? Carrie heard me hang up the phone.

"What did Dr. Ann say, David?" she asked. Her face literally changed from anger to sadness as I added each horrible detail of what this dog had experienced.

"What about Constantine? They obviously aren't going to get along," Carrie stated. "We can't do this, David. We just can't."

"Let's talk about it after I pick him up," I said.

By the time I brought the dog home, Carrie had Constantine on his leash in another room. The stray ran to her as soon as I opened the door. She rubbed his head and looked at me with exasperation. "David . . ."

"Let's put him in the garage tonight and talk about it in the morning," I said without letting her finish, hoping to come up with a solution that night.

Once Carrie made a nice bed from an old blanket in our garage and gave him some food, we went upstairs to our bedroom with Constantine close behind. There was a lot to think about.

Only Constantine got a good night's sleep. Carrie and I tossed and turned, woke up, talked about it, and tried to get some sleep. By the time the sun rose, we believed we had a good solution.

We would give the dog a couple of weeks to see how things went between him and Constantine. It was touchy at first, especially around dinnertime until we began feeding them at different times. It worked for a couple of days, but then the fights started again. We had to walk them separately. We had to keep them in separate rooms. The dog continued sleeping in the garage. We tried not to get attached; we hadn't even named him because we weren't sure if he would adjust.

After two weeks, we decided we needed expert help. I called a trainer a friend of mine used for his disobedient dog. After telling the trainer about the dog, she suggested I bring him in for an assessment.

Just as Dr. Ann had surmised, this dog was sweet to humans. Getting along with other dogs was another story, but the trainer said she could work with him and Constantine together. Carrie only agreed to keep him after the trainer assured her she would guarantee the dogs would accept each other or she'd return our money.

It was only a few weeks before Constantine and the dog not only tolerated each other, but actually became playmates. His condition improved greatly. His hair grew in, covering most of the scarring, and his frame filled out. Carrie finally agreed to keep him.

When I suggested we name him Rudy Ruettiger after the famous Notre Dame football player known for his courageous, resilient spirit, Carrie said she couldn't think of a more apt name for our newest family member.

Dog's Best Friend

Shirley Jones

Mention the name Shirley Jones and you'll conjure images of the girl next door, a singing beauty from *Oklahoma!* and *Carousel*, a sultry prostitute in *Elmer Gantry*, or, as she is probably best known, the single mom with the singing children in the television series *The Partridge Family*. She has been a screen and stage actor for decades.

A little-known movie made for television that was shown on the Lifetime channel in 1997 starred Shirley Jones and Richard Mulligan. It was entitled *Dog's Best Friend*.

For years, Shirley has lived up to that name by giving homeless dogs a safe, loving home.

Her son Patrick Cassidy also carries on the tradition. In the summer of 1995, he went to one of Los Angeles's kill shelters to get a puppy for his children. They adopted a little two-month-old terrier/poodle mix, whom they named Hana, and they loved her.

However, within weeks of bringing the puppy home, Patrick was given the starring role in the U.S. touring company production of *Joseph and the Amazing Technicolor Dreamcoat*. His wife and children were going on tour with him, but knew the road was no place to care for a puppy.

"When Patrick asked if I would care for Hana while they were gone, I immediately agreed," Shirley said.

It was an easy decision. Shirley and her husband, Marty Ingels, loved dogs and she thought it would only be for a short time.

"Hana loved the large yard behind our home and she had the run of our house. She added so much fun to our lives. I even taught her to sing! I kept telling myself not to get too used to having her because there would come a day soon when I'd have to give her back," Shirley remembered.

Between the tour and other contractual obligations, Patrick had no suitable place for the puppy during this time. When the tour ended two years later, he asked for the puppy that was now a full-grown dog.

Shirley refused and said, "Absolutely not. I'm too attached. Hana is my girl now." And that was that. Patrick knew his mom. There was no changing her mind.

A year later, Shirley decided to visit a Los Angeles shelter to get a playmate for Hana.

She saw a handsome golden retriever and asked why the dog hadn't been adopted. "Oh, but he has been. Twice. Each time the dog was returned because the owners thought he was untrainable," said the manager.

When the dog was brought out of his cage, he stood tall and confident. Shirley could not imagine what was wrong with the dog. He appeared very healthy and she was told the dog had a clean bill of health.

The manager offered a little more history. "He was raised in China and even has a passport in his name, Kingbo."

Shirley had had golden retrievers before and liked the breed. She adopted the dog on the spot and brought him home. She decided to shorten his name to King. It suited him.

When Shirley introduced King to Hana, he took one look at her and ran as fast as he could toward the pool. And then jumped in. He stayed there until Marty took Hana back into the house.

"It was a strange meeting. It was only the first indication that this golden was different," Shirley explained. "We tried teaching him the basic commands: heel, come, fetch. But he didn't respond."

They hired a trainer who got the same response—actually it was no response. The trainer asked if the dog's ears had been tested and Shirley assured him he could hear. In fact, he could hear so well that if he was outside and she quietly tore open the bag with his food in it, he would come running through the doggy door as if his life depended on it.

No, his hearing wasn't the problem. Marty wondered if it was because the dog had been raised in China and asked, "Do we have to learn how to speak Chinese now?"

The lightbulb lit. He didn't understand English. Now they understood why the previous owners brought him back and thought he couldn't be trained.

Slowly, King began to respond to their commands, but they had to repeat them over and over, and show him what action they wanted him to take. It was like teaching a child another language. The more they worked with him, the quicker he understood.

Shirley found the best way to train him was with food. "He is a good dog, but eats everything in sight. And not just his and Hana's dog food, either. He eats rocks, twigs, their toys, rope, and an occasional piece of clothing. He must have a cast-iron stomach because nothing he eats seems to bother him," she stated.

Hana is Shirley's sweet girl. She cuddles up next to her when she is sitting and follows her around the yard while she is gardening. King, on the other hand, is curious and likes to dig and bury things in the middle of her carefully planted flower beds. He will take off running after imaginary squirrels or rabbits like Don Quixote battling the windmills. King definitely marches to his own drummer. Between King and Hana's singing it is like an all-new canine Partridge Family.

The Good, the Bad, and the Bean

Jamie-Lynn Sigler

Many people know Jamie-Lynn Sigler as Tony Soprano's daughter, Meadow, on *The Sopranos*. Like her dad, Meadow was sassy, troubled, and a tough cookie in more ways than one.

However, that was just a role. The real Jamie-Lynn is a huge animal lover, and has a soft spot for homeless animals.

"I believe in rescuing an animal rather than purchasing one because there are so many who need loving, safe homes," Jamie-Lynn began. "I went to the Los Angeles animal control shelter not really knowing what kind of dog to adopt. I wanted to see if I had a connection with any of them."

Jamie-Lynn knew this was a high-kill shelter housing many loving dogs and cats just waiting to be adopted by loving people. She was prepared to be overwhelmed no matter what shelter she visited, but she did not let that keep her from opening her heart and home to one of those strays.

As she rounded a corner, her eyes were met with the most soulful hazel eyes she had ever seen. When she asked the staff member to tell her about the puppy, the woman told her she believed the puppy was about eleven weeks old and a Havanese and, maybe, wheaten/terrier mix. "He was so affectionate and plastered

my face with puppy kisses. I fell in love," Jamie-Lynn said.

She was told the puppy was adopted at eight weeks old and spent two weeks with another owner who had wanted an outside dog. The poor puppy was tied to a tree and left to fend for himself in battling the elements. During that time, there were torrential rains and cold nights. The owner never bothered providing a doghouse or thought of bringing the puppy into his home.

At the beginning of the third week, the owner noticed the puppy was coughing and wheezing and wasn't eating or drinking. It had lost a lot of weight and was very lethargic.

Instead of caring for the puppy or returning it to the shelter from where he adopted him, the owner brought him to a shelter close to his home. The puppy was near death and this despicable owner did not want to deal with him. A veterinarian at the shelter determined the puppy had an advanced case of pneumonia, and was severely dehydrated and malnourished. They immediately began treatment.

Jamie-Lynn was so thankful she had come when she did. It had been a week since the puppy was returned and he was on the road to recovery.

"When I asked to hold the puppy, he immediately responded to my touch. He was playful and affectionate," Jamie-Lynn remembered. "I sat in the hall while feeding him treats. After introducing myself, we hit it off as if we were old friends. I called to him and he responded quickly. The way he bounded over to me looked like he was a little jumping bean. I decided to name him Bean, a wise decision indeed as it fits his personality to a tee."

It took her twenty minutes to complete the adoption papers. She was told she had to get Bean the next day after the vet neutered and microchipped him. "I could hardly sleep that night knowing that the following day I would have a handsome gray-and-white, fluffy puppy to love," she continued.

When Jamie-Lynn arrived the next afternoon, the staff presented Bean to her along with his license, new puppy sweater, a tennis ball, and a bag of nutritious puppy food. "All I had to do was add the love," Jamie-Lynn said.

And she had plenty to give.

She continued, "As he settled into his new home, I discovered Bean loves having his picture taken. You would think he was practicing to be a model in *Vogue* the way he poses whenever he sees a camera."

"When I got pregnant, Bean was a great comfort, especially on days when I was stressed about becoming a mother. I think he was there to remind me how much love I have to share," she said.

For the next few months, Bean's personality got bigger, as did Jamie-Lynn's midriff. He became calmer and more protective around her. On their daily runs, instead of trying to break the sound barrier, he walked obediently by her side at a much slower pace, for which Jamie-Lynn was thankful.

"The closer it came time to deliver, the more patient Bean became. It was amazing. It was as if he knew our lives were going to change," Jamie-Lynn said.

Once Beau was born, Bean revealed another facet of his personality. He adopted Beau as his brother and watches closely as Jamie-Lynn cares for her newborn. "Bean never misses a chance to give doggy kisses to Beau or jump into the picture when we're taking one of the baby. He's such a ham," she concluded.

Jamie-Lynn and her fiancé, Cutter, adore their boys!

From Mexico with Love

Adrienne Barbeau

Adrienne Barbeau came to prominence as Rizzo, the tough, but endearing leader of the Pink Ladies in the 1970s Broadway play *Grease*. She is probably best known as Carol Traynor, the divorced daughter of Maude Findlay, played by Bea Arthur, in the sitcom *Maude*.

What most people do not know is that she is a dog lover. When one of her teenage sons asked for a Siberian husky as a birthday present, Adrienne got him the cutest puppy she could find. He named her Chloe.

Adrienne had done a lot of research about the breed, but had no idea the puppy would be so destructive. Chloe quickly developed some bad habits. She ate shoes (usually the most expensive), demolished furniture (the new sofa), chewed up a video camera (one of her sons left it on his bedroom floor), and tore several books apart before Adrienne either started or finished reading them. Adrienne decided to rescue a puppy as a playmate for Chloe.

"I drove to several animal shelters throughout Southern California until I discovered Adopt-a-Pet online. As soon as I entered 'golden retriever,' one of our choices, a picture of a stunning puppy appeared," Adrienne said.

Adrienne e-mailed the organization immediately and received an instant reply. They had just posted his picture online. Adrienne was the first to inquire about him.

She was told that a farmer found the puppy and the puppy's sister wandering

alone in a field in Ensenada, Mexico. Someone had abandoned them. They had no parents, no water, and were starving. The puppies had no shelter from the sweltering sun during the day or blankets to keep them warm during the cold nights. The farmer who spotted them contacted Animal Advocates of the United States, an organization with shelters for rescued dogs throughout Mexico and Southern California.

The puppies immediately were picked up by Animal Advocates, and after treating them for malnutrition and dehydration, mange, and an infestation of fleas, it was determined they were about two months old. Both received the appropriate vaccinations. After a few weeks, they were given a clean bill of health. Their lives were saved.

The puppies were sent to foster homes in Mexico until they were old enough to be neutered. While they gained weight and began to thrive, the organization began to look for forever homes. Adrienne learned the male puppy had been transferred to a foster home in Corona, California.

Adrienne believes it was no coincidence that the head of the organization had an appointment the next day in Studio City, which was close to her home. The woman offered to bring the puppy to Adrienne to see how he did as a companion for Chloe. If they didn't get along, the woman would take him back to his foster home that evening.

Adrienne was a bit nervous about the dogs' first meeting. Chloe was used to getting all the attention. She was the alpha in the house when friends' dogs came to visit. Adrienne had no idea what to expect from the puppy.

When the woman parked, she took the puppy from the backseat of her car. Adrienne put a leash on Chloe and both women kept their fingers crossed. They approached each other and the dogs met.

After the usual sniffing, the male puppy rolled onto his back to which Chloe put her paw on the puppy's tummy to let him know who was boss. As soon as she lifted her paw, the puppy ran around her in circles and then flipped over onto his back again, wanting to play some more. Needless to say, the meeting was a success.

The next step was to bring both dogs to her sons' school to get their opinion. Adrienne got to the school during their lunch hour. When the boys saw the puppy, they ran over and played with both dogs. And that was that. There was no question about keeping him. The boys came up with the name Little Bear because he looked like a teddy bear. He was little with soft fur and he had big brown eyes and was cute and cuddly.

Her sons asked if they could skip the rest of their school day and go home with their new puppy, but Adrienne said there would be plenty of time to get acquainted.

"The boys were so excited and promised to take care of the new puppy," Adrienne said.

After dinner as the boys prepared to do their homework, Chloe ran off with one of their books and Little Bear took off in the opposite direction with a notebook. "Next thing we knew, there was paper flying in two rooms as if they were training for a synchronized Olympic event, paper shredding," Adrienne remembered. "Like the old excuse, the dogs literally ate the boys' homework."

Her plan on having them play together was not going as well as expected. Over the next few weeks, Chloe and Little Bear took turns to see who could dig the deepest hole in her garden, who could chew up the most soccer socks, who could bark the loudest, and who could get the most attention in the house. Most days it was a tie.

"Our biggest problem, and something I didn't realize, is that golden retrievers are very possessive of their person, and I am his person! Little Bear is not happy when I give Chloe any attention, he wants me all to himself. Both dogs are loving and gentle, although Chloe might have a different opinion. She and Little Bear usually end the evening with an all-out tug-of-war with someone's pajamas or socks or one of my bras," Adrienne reported.

"Our lives are anything but boring!"

Bronco, Desilu, Gabe, and Emmy

They Could No Longer Run

Erin and George Pennacchio

George Pennacchio is the entertainment reporter for ABC7 *Eyewitness News*. He is also host of ABC7's *Evening at the Academy Awards Pre-Show* and *Post-Show*. During his broadcasting career, George has won three Emmy Awards for his work. He and his wife, Erin, appropriately named one of their beloved rescued greyhounds Emmy.

On a rainy day back in early 1997, George and Erin trekked to a greyhound rescue about forty miles from their home. Since George is highly allergic to many breeds of dogs, a friend had suggested that they look into this rescue organization, because greyhounds are hypoallergenic and there are so many of them coming off the tracks when they either retire or get injured, that it is hard to place them all.

They went to the greyhound rescue to see if George would be okay around them. As they walked into the room with all the retired racers up for adoption, there was one old guy who didn't even bother to get up. He'd been passed over enough. Naturally, he was the one!

So, a ninety-pound, eight-year-old named Bronco suddenly became part of their family.

"We weren't even prepared for him," George said. "We stopped at the pet store on the way home and bought food, dog bowls, and a big dog bed. When we set the bed down on the family room floor, Bronco jumped right in and stayed there for hours. He was home."

Smart as a whip, he required no house-training. Bronco just wanted to be someone's pet. "There were visible scars on his body from an abusive past, but he left those scars behind, willing to trust us from the moment he walked into our lives," George remembered.

On Bronco's ninth birthday, they decided it was time to give him some company. They alerted the rescue that they would be coming back to get Bronco a partner. They decided it would be best for Bronco to choose his new friend himself. He was rather picky, though. It took three trips before he chose Desilu to become a part of their family. "The signs they clearly show when they like one another is that they meet and kind of run off together and can't stop playing and showing off for each other. When they are not interested, they barely acknowledge each other. Sometimes they flirt with more than one, but usually they just favor one in the end," Erin said.

From day one, Bronco and Desilu were inseparable.

"When Bronco passed, Desilu cried for days. While we weren't ready yet for another dog, Desilu was so sad and lonely that we put her needs ahead of ours and headed back to the rescue a couple of months later. Desilu fell in love with Billy, and so did we, discovering what an amazing, loyal, and silly boy he was. That's when we knew love was greater than loss and that when rescued dogs pass on, they allow another one to experience a life being truly loved," George said softly.

Gabe, their current boy, is now a senior who chose the much younger and very silly Emmy to share his life in their home. They're quite a pair.

George and Erin haven't been without a retired racer since the moment Bronco entered their lives eighteen years ago. "We've always let our greyhounds select their partners. So far, every match has been great," says George.

Princess Fiona

Chris and Michele Gentry

Somewhere in South Los Angeles, not far from the intersection of Garbage Street and Graffiti Way, there is an old body shop. Behind its crumbly cement block walls covered in graffiti, there is a pile of trash: rotten food in moldy wrappers, a soccer ball, an old broom, newspapers, a rusty rake, and other assorted filth. A throwaway dog once called this home.

Did this discarded animal wonder, "Why am I out here? Where are my humans?" Did she ask what was going on or where she was? There were no answers. Only constant hunger, isolation, and fear. Only the unrelenting noise of traffic and people passing by, and the occasional drenching when it rained.

She can't tell us how she ended up there and survived those mean streets, or for how long. Maybe some kind soul from the neighborhood gave her food and water. Somehow, she managed. Months, maybe years of ground-in grime in her matted fur served as protective coloration, and she successfully blended in with her surroundings. She was almost invisible. But not completely.

Eldad Hagar and his wife, Audrey, have eagle-eye vision. Their keen vision was developed over the ten years since they'd founded the Hope for Paws rescue organization. Alerted by their friend Mary Chatman, a member of their rescue network, the couple went in search of the helpless stray. After looking around the nasty fenced-in area behind the shop, the rescuers had their doubts. They saw nothing in the way of a lost dog on that damp and drizzly day in 2011. Perhaps the dog had wandered off.

Then, in an instant of inspired sight, Audrey spotted movement. There, above the putrid pile of filth and trash, a pair of staring eyes in a grimy and matted little animal head slowly appeared. Homeless, tagless, and sightless, the poodle mix did not yelp or growl or move.

In this case, it wasn't "fight or flight"; it was "freeze." As Audrey's hand gently reached out to this small and starving pup, it was as wide-eyed as a deer in the headlights. The dog's only movement was to urinate on herself in total terror.

The rescuers took turns softly stroking the dog's head and face. Their reassuring voices tried to tell her she was safe. Tears ran down Audrey's cheeks as she gathered up the little dog in a blanket. Eldad, video camera in one hand and gently coaxing with the other, recorded the rescue. The threesome got in the car and left that place forever. And, on the ride home, in another inspired vision, Audrey just knew this dog's name: Princess Fiona.

By the time they got home, it was clear to her rescuers that Fiona was completely blind. By what miracle had she survived? "She looked so defeated, she was trembling, frightened, and exhausted," Eldad recalls. They shaved Fiona to the skin to liberate her from the mass of matted and filthy fur, and then bathed her to clear up the worst case of flea infestation they'd ever seen. Later, the rescue team took her to Dr. Michael Chang, a vet specializing in eye surgery. He determined that with a lens implant in her right eye, Fiona's sight could be partially saved. But the cost was prohibitive.

The Hagars take videos of all their rescue efforts, and Fiona's turned out to be especially good. They posted it on the Internet, and the video went viral. Countless people in countless locales all over the world pitched in. Miraculously, the $4,000 needed for the surgery was donated by kind souls all over the world. The operation was a success, and Fiona now sees.

Some say there are no coincidences. Of the million hits from all over the world, it was right there in Los Angeles, virtually in the Hagars' own backyard, where someone felt compelled to connect more deeply with Fiona. Michele Gentry, adoptive mother of three rescue poodle-mix girls, sobbed uncontrollably as she watched the video. Then, she called her husband, Chris, to come and watch, too. Something about Fiona deeply resonated within Michele's heart. Maybe it was in her subconscious, but somehow she knew this was her own dogs' missing sister. After all, they looked so alike. That dog needed to be with her family. "I wanted Fiona to have the puppyhood she never had," Michele explained.

The Gentrys recall how amazed they were when they first met Fiona at the Hagars. "We couldn't believe how happy she was after all she'd been through," they said. Fiona had already learned to navigate her way around the furniture at the Hagars and knew how to play with their dogs even before her eye surgery. And here she was, welcoming Michele and Chris like family. The couple knew this dog was special. Fiona soon joined the Gentry family where she lives and plays happily ever after with her sisters, Lola, Ali, and Bella, under the watchful eyes of their loving parents.

Fiona, with her single eye, has taught so many to see with our hearts, the best and clearest way to see.

Fiona sees so well and is so smart that she has become a celebrity on TV talk shows. She also has many Facebook friends and gets her own fan mail. She is so insightful and wise that she knows *video* is Latin for "I see." Her inspiring story seems to be a nod to Dutch philosopher Erasmus's famous saying, though in Fiona's version it would be: "In the land of the blind, the one-eyed *dog* is *Princess*."

Package of Joy

Lisa Arturo

One evening as I was settling down to some quiet time at home with a good book, I received an urgent call from a close friend who is active in the rescue community in Los Angeles. She quickly explained that a pit bull/boxer mix named Olive Pit had been picked up in South Central a few weeks ago. When she had called earlier that evening to see if the dog had been adopted, she was told "Olive's time is up."

South Central happens to have one of the highest kill rates in the country. This means a dog can be euthanized within three days after it's impounded if the supervisor "gives the word." I immediately called the shelter to let them know I was on my way down to see Olive.

I arrived at the shelter within the hour and asked to see her. The manager took me to the back of the dark, cold kennel to the cage where she lay scared, shaking, and tail between her legs. As he unlocked the crate, I knelt down, trying not to frighten her, and waited to see what Olive would do.

It didn't take long before she slowly came out of her cage, close to the ground, almost crawling. We looked at each other for a moment. She must have known I meant her no harm. She stood, walked over, and licked my hand. Before I could even touch her, she quickly backed up, unsure of what my reaction would be.

When I smiled and spoke her name quietly, she immediately came back to me, although still cautious. She melted under the touch of my hand on her head.

My initial intention was to foster and find her a forever home. I had already saved and placed forty-seven dogs that year and vowed to do the same for Olive. I completed the paperwork as Olive sat quietly next to me, as if to prove she was a good girl and just wanted someone to take her home and love her.

The first night was difficult. She moaned while sleeping. Her body jerked as if she was trying to escape from something or someone. When she jerked, I gently rubbed her head to assure her she was in a safe place. By the second night, she slept soundly. I looked at this homeless animal that probably only wanted a safe place to live. She had no idea how much joy she had already brought to my life because of the unconditional love I felt from her.

After three days of good food and much-needed rest, Olive came out of her shell completely. After the abusive life she must have had until then, I was surprised to see how happy, playful, and very affectionate she was. She followed me from room to room, tail in a constant state of perpetual motion, making sure I didn't leave her alone. My heart ached at the thought of upsetting her again and leaving her in another home—even if it was a great home. I knew there was something special about Olive. Her soft brown eyes didn't reflect the tough life she had probably known. She was the epitome of joy wrapped up in a brown, white, and black package.

I decided to keep her.

The amazing thing about Olive is that she's always happy. Most dogs become frightened when they know they're going to the vet. Not Olive. She happily jumps into the car and even plays with the vet when she enters the examining room. I think it's because Olive knows she will be coming back home with me. I've earned her trust. She has my unconditional love.

What really amuses me is even when I think she's sound asleep on her bed, somehow she knows when I glance her way because her tail starts wagging. She'll then open one eye as if to say, "I caught you looking!"

She has taught me to smile even when I'm having a really bad day. She can sense my moods and knows when I need a "dog hug" or want to celebrate good news. She also knows when she's done something naughty because I'll stand with my hands on my hips and say, "Olive Pit, what have you done?" She immediately lowers her head and lies down. However, she'll soon see everything is forgiven by the smile on my face.

When we go to the dog park, Olive somehow finds the most timid dogs and brings them out of their shells. Within minutes, she'll have them running after her full speed. She has a way of doing that with people, too.

Pit bulls have a bad reputation and when some people see me walking with Olive, they will actually get off the sidewalk and walk on the street. Even after I assure them Olive is friendly, many are still cautious. She'll then prove it by waiting for them to approach before licking their hand, wagging her tail, or rolling onto her back. She has changed many people's minds about what kind of dog a pit bull really is—loving, gentle, and ready to please!

Olive also helps with my foster puppy program at local animal shelters. She cares for the puppies as if they were her own. She becomes their surrogate mother as she washes them and watches over them. When she lies down, the puppies are drawn to her and cuddle close to her warm body, knowing she will protect them.

Many pit bull and boxer mixes don't end up with happy lives as Olive did. Some people adopt these types of dogs from shelters with no intention of loving them as pets. Instead, they use these precious dogs as "gladiators" that fight to the death. I constantly get e-mails about pits in need of urgent medical attention because they've been used as bait in dogfight rings. It's devastating to know some people pay to watch dogs tear each other apart for their amusement, especially after Michael Vick's convictions for dogfighting. One of my goals is to make people more aware this is still happening—and happening often!

As an actress and animal advocate, I am committed to educating the public about this beautiful, trustworthy breed, and how this heinous, illegal blood sport can no longer be tolerated.

Against the Odds

Lynn Kincaid

I t really was a dark and stormy, wintry night when Tito, a horse trainer who works on my ranch, drove to a casino because he felt lucky. He had really been looking forward to playing a few hands of blackjack. He was remembering his last visit and knew tonight was going to be different. Tonight he was going to win. And win big!

A storm was raging. Lightning lit up the evening sky, quickly followed by thunder rumbling loudly. Deep puddles were turning to ice throughout the parking lot. As Tito tried to find a puddle-free parking spot, he almost hit a mud-covered dog sitting next to a parked car, trying to find shelter from the storm.

He wondered briefly if the owner had left the dog outside of his car before it started raining. Then he remembered it had been raining all day. Tito's attention quickly turned to the lights of the casino and he didn't give the dog another thought. His mind began forming a winning strategy for the card tables.

After a couple of hours, he realized his luck was not going to change. It was just as bad, no, worse than on his last outing. He had to laugh when he thought of his lucky feeling as he mumbled to no one, "Lady Luck left me high and dry tonight."

As Tito left the casino, he noticed how much the temperature had dropped. It was no longer raining. It was starting to snow. Upon reaching his parking place, he saw the poor dog lying next to his truck on a patch of ice. The car was gone. He knelt to see if the dog had any tags, and what gender it was, and noticed the dog wasn't only drenched, it was freezing and covered in blood.

He carefully picked the female dog up. Tito stopped at an all-night grocery store and bought dog food, bandages, and antiseptic cream. When he reached his home, he inspected her more carefully. After bathing her, he decided he would tend to her wounds as best he could.

He wondered how long she had been homeless. He could tell she was weak from her ordeal. She obviously was malnourished. Her fur was matted and she looked like she had been in fights with other animals.

Still, she seemed friendly and waited patiently as he poured the dog food into a bowl. She ate every morsel as fast as she could and then drank the entire bowl-ful of water. He spread a blanket on the floor next to his bed. She took great pains to fluff it so that it was "just right." Just before he turned the lights out, he looked at her. She was looking up at him with deep gratitude in her sparkly brown eyes.

Tito fell asleep to the sound of the dog's gentle, rhythmic breathing.

The next morning, he checked her wounds and changed the dressing. They both ate a large breakfast and he decided not to take her to a shelter. Tito then called and told me about the stray. Since he lived in a small apartment, he knew he couldn't keep her, but he wanted to know if I was interested in seeing her. If I was, he could bring her to work with him. I immediately said, "Yes!"

I was outside watching for his truck. The moment Tito drove through the gate to our ranch, I could see the dog's head outside the window, ears flapping in the wind. As soon as he opened the door, and she jumped out of his truck, I knew she was home. I believe she did, too, as she quickly ran to meet my other dogs, Jake, Toffee, and Madison. After the required sniffing, they accepted her immediately into their pack and off they went. It was hard for her to keep up with them; she was limping.

I took her to the vet and he stitched her wounds and gave her antibiotics.

Within days, she was much better and gave the other dogs a real run for their money. Jennifer, my daughter, named her Tess, and was happy we finally had a female dog. They adopted each other!

Ours is a working ranch and Tess had to learn the job the other dogs have, herding the horses. She was made for this job and takes it quite seriously. While the boys want to play, Tess doesn't stop until the horses are safely in the corral. As soon as I close the gate, she knows her job is done and she joins the others running free, swimming in the lake, and napping in the sunshine. Her favorite job, though, is greeting visitors to our ranch who board their horses or come for riding and jumping lessons, and she welcomes them with a wagging tail.

My daughter, Jennifer, has special needs and Tess is now her wonderfully helpful sidekick that she loves so much. When Jennifer comes home from school, Tess greets her at the gate and carries her backpack. While doing her homework, one of Jennifer's hands is busy typing on the computer keyboard while the other is lovingly rubbing Tess's head. Tess doesn't leave her side until Jennifer is safely tucked into her bed and gives Tess a last rub and kiss on the head.

Once Tess has patrolled the house and is satisfied all is well, she fluffs her doggy bed next to Jennifer's bed and lies down peacefully, always keeping a watchful eye and ear ready to see and hear any strange noise.

Every weekday morning, Tess waits by the door for Jennifer to finish breakfast and grab her lunch bag and books. They walk to the school bus stop and wait. Once my daughter is safely on the bus, Tess starts her full day of herding, running, swimming, napping, and greeting.

Tess knows when it's time for the school bus to bring Jennifer home and stops whatever she's doing to run to the bus stop. Then Tess begins her nightly ritual of eating dinner, getting homework rubs, patrolling the house, fluffing her bed, and finally guarding my daughter.

When Tito and I speak about the evening he saved Tess, I always remind him how lucky we all were. He won by taking Tess home, caring for her, and finding her a great home. Tess won a family who really loves her. My daughter won a special friend. My boys won a member of their pack that keeps them moving. My husband and I won a wonderful addition to our family. Tito may have thought Lady Luck abandoned him that evening, but it turned out to be one of the luckiest nights for my family!

Lucky Lady

Rescued at Sea

John and Michele Lissberger

The Pacific seas were getting rougher off the coast of the Mexican Baja Peninsula, somewhere near Ensenada. At the helm of their fifty-foot yacht, John Lissberger negotiated the swells as his wife, Michele, stood watch. By some miracle, she saw in the distance a pair of black pointy ears bobbing up and down in the waves.

"At first, I thought it was a harbor seal," Michele remembered. Then, to her horror, she realized this was no marine animal; it was a dog, water-logged and struggling to stay afloat. Michele alerted her husband. With a quick change in course, he aimed the yacht directly at the canine being tossed around in the high seas. They watched the poor dog paddle for its life for at least a nautical mile before John was able to bring the yacht close enough for an attempted rescue.

The couple's dalmatian, Dash, raced up and down the prow barking loudly as if to encourage his drowning comrade to stay afloat. Michele weighed anchor as John quickly prepared the dinghy for the dangerous job at hand. The both knew fishing the dog out of the breaking waves was going to be risky and difficult. The dinghy could tip over at any moment, throwing them into the same dangerous situation from which they were trying to rescue the dog. Nevertheless, these dog lovers knew in their heart it was something they had to do.

Dash jumped into the dinghy right after Michele. The powerful swells challenged their every attempt to rescue the visibly exhausted dog. The seas tossed their tiny craft around like a cork. With one arm grasping a side of the small boat and the other tightly wrapped around Dash, Michele kept her eyes focused on the dog that was now taking longer to surface each time the sea pulled it under. John fought the waves to steer the dinghy closer to the dog. The Pacific seemed to be howling, "No, you can't have her!"

Dash looked at Michele from the dinghy's floor. His big-eyed stare seemed to plead, "We can't leave without my comrade. You must try again!"

Finally, John was close enough to reach into the cold water and grab the dog by the long fur on its neck as it was on its way down again. The dinghy began to tip. Michele and Dash counterbalanced John's weight on the other side of the small craft. John heaved the drenched creature up and over the side into the dingy. A terrified, exhausted black-and-white dog lay at their feet, gasping for air. She was a female and visibly shuddering from the cold and shock. Luckily, they had brought towels and a blanket to dry and wrap her in on their way back to the yacht.

Michele still shudders when she recalls, "We didn't know if the poor little angel had been swept overboard, or worse, someone deliberately threw her overboard. She had no collar. There was no sign of a doggy life jacket."

After a few moments, they inspected the severely neglected and abused female shepherd mix. Luckily, there was no sign of injuries. However, she was a real shipwreck.

They tried to locate her owner by checking with local marinas, hailing nearby craft on the radio, and even contacting local veterinarians. No one had heard of any reports of a lost dog.

The dog's rescue at sea continued on land as Michele and John took her to a veterinarian for inoculations and a checkup. He advised the couple to take the dog to the United States and put her in a shelter. How could they do this? Her fate was certainly to be put down or abandoned again. She would surely end her days in misery and isolation. Hadn't this poor dog suffered enough for one lifetime?

Michele and John made their new passenger comfortable and warm. She ate a little, but slept most of the time on their way home to San Diego, California. During the trip, they fell in love with this friendly pup. The thought of leaving her to a worse fate weighed heavily on them. They decided to keep her if she and Dash got along. By the time they arrived home, Dash was in love with her, too.

The couple knew the dog's luck had changed. Not only did she survive the deadly high seas, but Lady Luck also saw to it that Michele would miraculously spot her and John would be able to maneuver the dinghy to rescue her. And how lucky, too, that she would be rescued by devoted dog lovers. That is why Michele and John decided to call her Lucky Lady, and then just Lady for short.

However, shortly after her homecoming, Lady's luck turned again. She couldn't stop shaking and became seriously ill. The vet said it was because of severe exposure to the elements. Through months of intensive treatment and lots of love, Lady eventually was able to regain her strength and health. This time her good luck stayed with her. She finally hit the lottery.

Lady lives in a secluded desert hideaway with a lake comfortably with John, Michele, and Dash. Most days, Lady loves running free on the golf course with Dash or riding peacefully with John in his golf cart. When the family stays at their mountain cabin, they hike together for hours. On some weekends, when the family goes to the beach, Lady, now a confirmed landlubber, is content to let the others swim as she lays in the shade under the large umbrella on her special blanket.

Not long ago, their beloved Dash passed on and Lady fills the huge void in their hearts he left behind. Michele still marvels when she looks down at their rescue dog snoozing on a down pillow in the warm spot next to the window, with no cares in the world. When asked how Lady came to them, Michele starts by saying, "She is the Salty Dog that became a Lucky Lady." She ends the story by repeating what they say in that famous dog food commercial, "All you add is love." And Michele quickly adds, "And, a little bit of luck!"

43

The Pet Rescue Center

Christine Madruga

I started rescuing animals at a very young age. What motivated me was that I was raised by my family to love everything and everybody.

Early on, my friend Lexi and I rescued two German shepherd puppies that were just two months old out of our neighbor's backyard. We'd learned that the puppies were suffering from exposure due to the hot La Quinta desert sun, because they were being kept outside, without enough food and water, and we just knew that we had to save them. So we scrambled over the fence and rescued them. They would be safe with us, and we named them Lucy and Zolly.

Then my family moved to Long Beach, California, where there were many animals on the streets. The homelessness there touched my heart, and I would go out to find little baby kittens, cats, and stray dogs, and bring them home with me. I grew up and went off to attend college, and my passion for animals went with me. On my way to my classes at College of the Desert, I started bringing food with me to feed the feral cats. And then, you guessed it: I was quick to bring these cats in need home to my little house in the desert.

And this is the story that turned my life. One windy day, one of the playful cats crawled up in-between the fan and radiator of my car, and I didn't know it, and when the engine turned over Blackie was trapped and hurt. I rushed her to the vet where miraculously her leg was saved, and a new path for my life opened up right before me. What happened is that since I didn't have the funds to pay the vet bills, I was able to make a quick deal with Dr. Jackson to pay off the costs by working in the kennels. And this developed a career for me.

I absolutely loved being in close contact with the animals, and I loved witnessing—while peeking through the surgery room's glass door—the awe-inpiring surgeries that would heal these sweet beings. Dr. Jackson took notice of my interest, and soon after, he asked me to come in and help him during a Sunday emergency. It was at that moment that realization hit me: I decided that I wanted to dedicate my life to providing care and shelter for helpless animals. School became secondary, much to the dismay of my family, and I never looked back as I became wrapped up in the mission that I felt provided me with a purposeful life.

I grabbed with gusto every opportunity to learn all the skills that would help me run the business side of a practice, such as reading X-rays, ordering lab work, and client comforting. I was like a sponge trying to soak up everything that I could. A new veterinarian named Gary soon joined the practice, and we inspired each other. For years we provided treatment to the city and county animal control centers for strays that were picked up on the streets. Sadly, those same animals that we cared for were then released to shelters, most of which were kill shelters that had a time limit for keeping them.

This awful cycle raised my hackles, and I could no longer stand to be a part of this sad story. In March 1998, I founded The Pet Rescue Center. I only had four cages to house the animals at that time, and I worked tirelessly because it mattered.

I got the nonprofit requirements in place, and I was off and running. The journey had begun. Quickly, I made appointments with surrounding city officials and pleaded with them to give The Pet Rescue Center the prescribed $40 fee that they were currently paying as an impound fee to the county shelters. I promised that with those funds, I would get the dogs and cats vaccinated, spayed or neutered, microchipped, and, best of all, my newly formed center would find new forever homes for these lovable pets.

Now we have a home for our center in a new site that was purchased in 2006. To date, over 9,000 dogs and 7,062 cats have gotten care and shelter, and we have given them a new lease on life by finding homes for them. Schools have opened their doors for me to educate kids on the importance of spaying and neutering to control the animal population. I have experienced taking dogs out of shelters on their last day scheduled for life, and in many cases, minutes before they "went in the other room" to be killed.

Being able to give the gift of life to these innocent animals has been one of the most profound and greatest joys in my life!

Hairy Houdini

Andrea Greeven Douzet

The French citizens celebrate July 14 as Bastille Day, the day the common people stormed the Bastille prison as part of their independence from the monarchy.

On July 14, 2012, another day of freedom was celebrated at an event put on by Last Chance Animal Rescue in New York. It was on this day that Andrea Greeven Douzet and her twin girls, Gabi and Gigi, first saw Bell, a beautiful golden retriever/shar-pei mix that was there to be adopted by a loving family.

Marcy, who hosted the event at her home, told Andrea and her daughters as much as she could about Bell's history.

The dog's first name was Purdy. She was born on June 20, 2010, in North Carolina in a county known for an abundance of homeless, unneutered dogs, and kill shelters. The puppy ended up in one of them and, thankfully, was rescued by a volunteer that brought her to a shelter in New York City that focuses on finding forever homes for the animals.

An elderly couple had adopted the puppy to keep their young grandchildren amused when they visited. They named her Bell. Their grandchildren loved playing with the puppy and the puppy loved playing with them, too. However, the owners did not anticipate the amount of work and attention a puppy requires.

They tried for months to keep up with the puppy's demands, but decided the best thing for them—and the puppy—was to give her up for adoption. They brought the puppy to the Last Chance Animal Rescue with the hopes a family with younger children would adopt her.

The couple did the right thing, and that's where Bell's new life began.

"There was something about this particular dog that caught my girls' attention. She was extremely beautiful, with long flowing fur. However, the dog would not come when any of us called, but it was the way she wouldn't come that got our attention. She seemed to be playing a game of keep away that made her actions so adorable," Andrea began.

"It took a while for us to get close to Bell, but when we did, the girls begged me to adopt her. They didn't have to ask twice. On the way home, we tried thinking of a new name for the dog. Since I believed Purdy was the slang word for 'pretty' and the couple had misspelled the French word for pretty, we all agreed we should just add the 'e' at the end of her name," Andrea said.

Andrea had stopped on the way home and bought some doggy toys, a fluffy bed, and some treats in order to begin training Belle.

As soon as their car pulled into the driveway, the twins and the dog were ready for play. After an afternoon of fetch, Andrea noticed Belle seemed a little out of sorts. She would not eat her dinner. The next day, Andrea took Belle to the vet to have her checked out. "The vet said all the excitement from the day before caused Belle to have an upset stomach. He recommended we keep antacids just in case it happened again, which it does when the girls tire Belle out," Andrea continued.

Andrea also quickly discovered Belle is an experienced escape artist. She immediately learned how to burrow her way under the backyard fence at their home in Southampton. Andrea watched helplessly as Belle, true to her retriever bloodline, chased deer, seagulls, and squirrels around their rural neighborhood, as Andrea and the girls chased her and shouted her name in a futile effort to catch her.

While living in their New York City apartment, Belle learned how to unlock their sliding door and escaped by jumping off a second floor balcony in hot pursuit of pigeons and rats she had spotted.

"Belle could not be caught easily and was not interested in bribes of delicious treats as most dogs are. I think she thinks we are playing a game. She will stop running and let us get very close. Just as one of us is about to grab her collar, she bounds away, looking behind every once in a while to make sure we are still chasing her," Andrea said.

Andrea finally hired a professional dog trainer who worked with Belle throughout the summer. At first it was once a week, but because Belle was escaping every day, the trainer recommended training Belle every other day.

"When acting like her shar-pei side, Belle can be quite silly and rambunctious with large dogs she has encountered in our neighbors' yards. Once, a neighbor called to say Belle was in her yard and running with her dog's toys, and, was delighted when the dog chased after her. When the dog finally caught up with Belle, Belle rolled over onto her back, grabbed the dog's neck, and took it down like a professional wrestler. The neighbor was quite amused," Andrea reported.

Taking Belle for a walk was a chore. "I always had to be on the alert. If Belle saw a squirrel, bird, or another dog to chase, she would almost pull my arm out of the socket if I wasn't on guard. I had to hold onto her leash with both hands until the distraction flew or ran away. On the flip side of her personality, Belle would sit quietly for hours while the twins dressed her in a tutu, polished her toenails with red polish, or brushed her silky fur," she said.

The first year with Belle was difficult, yet full of fun. Belle eventually stopped escaping and learned to come when called, although every once in a while she slips back into "chase me" mode.

Andrea wrapped up by saying, "The girls and I were never bored with the mischief Belle got into inside or outside of our homes. She is extremely loving and an intelligent dog. She could figure out ingenious ways to escape no matter what precautions I took. I think she saw everything as a challenge—like she was a member of the Mission Impossible team. She is a lion and a teddy bear all rolled into one beautiful and regal dog. We cannot imagine our lives without her."

45   Madison

Sometimes a Hug Is All We Need

Christina Kirk

Nine years ago, my husband, Eric, and I lost our beautiful fawn-colored boxer to cancer. We decided almost immediately to rescue another boxer just like her. We returned to the boxer rescue center from where we had rescued her.

I walked a couple of the dogs, but felt no real connection with them. Then the manager brought Madison out. From where Eric and I sat, we could see she was a beautiful brindle brown-and-cream color. It also appeared she must have been abused based on the slight scarring on her body we could see even from a distance.

However, as the manager opened the swinging gate, the dog ran straight to me and jumped into my lap. This behavior caught me off guard, but before I could say anything, she wrapped her paws around my neck and nuzzled her head next to mine. The manager seemed surprised at her reaction to me and then told us the story of how she had come to the rescue center and the life of abuse she had suffered.

"A few weeks ago, Madison was found roaming the dangerous streets of South Central Los Angeles one evening by someone who almost ran her over," the manager said. The driver noticed she had no collar or identification and, thankfully, he called animal control and waited until they arrived. The dog was not easy to catch as she darted in and out of traffic until she was too exhausted to run anymore.

They took the stray to a nearby shelter that only kept dogs for three days before they are euthanized.

"Luckily, when the staff realized she was a pure-bred boxer, she was immediately transferred to our facility. The dog was severely underweight and had healed wounds on her face and back. She was missing fur on her legs, obviously from being in fights with other dogs. I surmised she must have been used as a pit bull fighter bait. Dogs that are used this way do not live long, so she must have escaped somehow. The vet thought she was about eighteen months old and said she already had a litter of puppies.

"Within the first week, we found her to be extremely aggressive to people and other dogs. We were not sure if anyone would want to adopt her. She has never reacted to anyone as she did with you."

I looked into Madison's big brown eyes, starving for love. She did not appear to be the same dog the manager had just described. As I rubbed her back, I said to Eric, "I think this dog just picked me."

As soon as I spoke those words, she jumped from my lap into his, again wrapping her paws in the same manner around his neck, nuzzling her mouth against his ears as if she wanted to whisper, "Take me home now, please!" It was unanimous and love at first sight for all three of us.

We adopted Madison that day.

She walked cautiously into our home and began sniffing everything in the foyer. We thought maybe she had caught the scent of the dog we had, but she did not seem to mind. She turned around as if to get permission from us to continue her investigation. When she saw us smiling, she walked into the next room. After she had checked the entire house, she finally jumped up on our bed, pulled the covers up around her head, and nestled it onto my pillow.

Within the first few days, we found Madison to be extremely affectionate and playful around small children, but quickly noticed some traits that made us worry. She was anxious and afraid around black males and other dogs—especially pit bulls. This made sense, considering what the manager told us about her background. We knew we had to do something about this quickly and hired a trainer who assured us that he could break her of these bad habits. He worked diligently with Madison for months and slowly we began to see real progress. It took not only consistent training, but also lots of love and patience on our part before Madison became rehabilitated, although she is still cautious around pit bulls.

Since then, I begin my day with a long run with Madison in the park. She loves to chase the ducks and geese around the pond, pulling me until I yell, "Heel" to regain control. Afterward, Madison loves riding in my car as I do my daily errands, her ears flapping wildly in the wind as her nose takes in the variety of smells in the city. She walks proudly by my side wherever we go. Her beautiful brindle fur is shiny. She loves the attention when people, even strangers, stop to pet her. She patiently waits for treats the shop owners have gotten into the habit of giving her, for being so good in their stores.

Eric works nights, so Madison is never alone and always has something to do. Just before he goes to work, he takes her for another run in our neighborhood. Two of my neighbors invite Madison over to play with their male dogs, keeping her busy many afternoons.

Since she is my bed partner, Madison nudges my arm and whines to wake me up in the middle of the night if she becomes uncovered. Many times I find myself pushed to the corner of the bed, and I have to regain my place by moving Madison reluctantly back to her side of the bed.

Even after nine years, Madison continues to greet Eric by jumping into his arms and wrapping her paws around his neck as she did on the first day we met. She loves when he cradles her in his arms like a baby. Since Madison is a healthy sixty-two pounds, she has learned to wait for me to kneel down so she can stand on her hind legs in order to wrap her paws around my neck, and then I scoop her up and hold her tight.

Madison is the love of our lives and enjoys the "good life." I am sure she has put the memory of her former life of abuse in one of the most dangerous neighborhoods in the country firmly behind her.

My Greatest Gift

Laura Chamberlin

Two years ago, I was very ill. As I recovered, I vowed if I stayed healthy for a year, I would rescue a dog as a gift to myself. As the months passed and my health continued to improve, I began looking seriously at shelter Web sites and researched different breeds.

Three days after getting a clean bill of health, Frank, a good friend, called because he knew about my plan to rescue a dog once I was healthy.

When I answered the phone, Frank said, "Earlier today, I saw a dog running down the road. Once I finally caught him, I called the phone number on his tag. When I brought the dog home, the owner said she had adopted him from a shelter three months earlier. She was told two former owners complained about him running away. Because the fence around her yard was high, she thought he wouldn't be able to get over it. But this was the fifth time he had escaped. She also has an older dog that injures itself trying to keep up with the little dog. When she asked if I knew anyone who was looking for a dog, I immediately thought of you. Can I bring you to meet him?"

"I'll go to meet him, Frank, but I'm not making any promises," I said.

We went to the owner's home. As soon as she answered the door, I saw this terrier-looking dog wagging his tail, sitting by her side. "This is Marley," she said.

He looked up at her when she said his name, then swung his head toward me as if he expected me to introduce myself.

I fell in love instantly. I could tell all he wanted was love and attention. I bent over and picked him up and was holding him in my arms when the woman said if I didn't take him she was going to bring him back to the shelter. I left with him that day.

When I brought Marley home, the first thing I did was change his name. He didn't look like a Marley. He looked like a . . . a . . . Spencer. I tried it out to see if he liked it.

"Spencer. Spencer, come," I said as I patted my thighs.

With the first "Spencer," his ears perked up. With the second, he ran straight to me, jumped into my arms, and gave me kisses all over my face and neck. I took that as his approval.

When I had him checked out at the vet, he said Spencer was a Tibetan terrier. When I researched the breed known as the "Holy Dog of Tibet," I discovered monks kept them as good luck charms and companions.

From the first day, Spencer was well-behaved—when I was around. It was a different story when I left him alone during the first few months. The first time, he figured out how to open my kitchen pantry and had a great time ripping open a box of cornmeal and shaking its contents all over the kitchen. The second time, Spencer found another cabinet to open and did the same thing to a box of quinoa. To this day, I'm still finding seeds in the strangest places. His next target was a box of oatmeal he managed to sprinkle all over my living room carpet. Finally, he tired of the kitchen and changed rooms. This time, Spencer finagled his way into a bathroom cabinet. When I arrived home, I discovered Spencer had TP'd each room by using twelve rolls of newly purchased toilet paper. This mess took me two hours to pick up. In each instance, he would slink behind the couch to hide. I think those were tests to make sure I wouldn't take him back to the pound. Obviously I passed the test. Since the toilet paper incident, he has been the perfect dog.

Spencer is friendly with everyone—especially children. We take a walk most mornings and usually meet one of my neighbors, a young mother and her three-year-old son, Tommy, riding his tricycle to preschool. Spencer gets excited when he sees Tommy, but waits patiently for the little boy to dismount his trike before giving Tommy slobbery kisses. Tommy giggles and hugs Spencer. I think they both look forward to their daily encounter.

Sometimes I think Spencer is more little boy than dog. There isn't a puddle he can resist. As soon as he spots one, he picks up speed and jumps into it, splashing wildly, getting as wet as he can, something like Gene Kelly did in his brilliant "Singin' in the Rain" dance number.

Spencer also has an unusual taste in doggy toys. His favorite is the obnoxious rubber chicken. I swear he's so addicted to it there must be some kind of dognip hidden in its belly. When I buy one, he immediately pounces on the bag to dig it out. None last very long; I have a drawer full of various chicken parts. Once I came home from work to find one in my bed, covers pulled up to its chin, and its head resting on my pillow. I sometimes think he loves the rubber chicken more than he loves me.

He is also a great networker. I've met almost all my neighbors because of Spencer's friendliness. He walks up to strangers, sits down in front of them, then rolls over. He believes everyone deserves the privilege of petting and getting to know him. I call him the mayor of the neighborhood.

I recently took care of my friend's dog that is blind and diabetic. Spencer was so caring with her. If she started to walk into the wall or furniture, he would gently guide her away from the obstacle. He sensed she couldn't play fetch, but once he discovered she was a great match in a rousing game of tug-of-war, they played for hours. If she needed to go out at night, Spencer would come to my bed and moan, a different moan than when he needed to go. They were great friends, unless he felt I was giving her too much attention. Then he would come between us and bark as if to say, "What about me?"

Spencer brought joy into my life and is true to his breed. He is my good luck charm, a great companion, and the greatest gift I ever received.

47 Shasta, Echo, Graham, and
Marina

Never Too Old to Fall in Love

Heather Schmidt

I didn't grow up with dogs, and although I have always been a person with a big heart in general, it was somewhat surprising to me that I became such a huge dog lover. I wouldn't have expected that I would one day live in my home with four large dogs, a cat, and a fish! No matter how old you are, you can fall in love with dogs.

My husband also never had any pets, so I introduced him to living with them. Now his own love and affection has grown for our pet family, and he has developed an incredibly strong bond with each of our kids and loves them as much as I do!

Shasta, our husky puppy that we rescued, was having some emotional issues that were causing some behavioral problems we needed to address. We met Gabi, who is a spiritual healer, at our friends' Christmas party, and they told me that Gabi was very successful working with animal behavioral and health problems. I became immediately intrigued with the possibility that she could help Shasta.

After the first session, Shasta tremendously improved, and I was delighted. Gabi is a connected energy healer and she focuses positive energy in a fashion to heal and transform in remarkable ways. Now, with each new addition, we depend upon Gabi's insightful contributions to our dogs' well-being.

I am a professional pianist and composer. I have a big grand piano in my living room and when I play it my first dog that I rescued, Echo—a female husky mix, who is our biggest husky of all—takes a pose and then howls as if she is singing her song for me! I saw Echo online on Petfinder, and I immediately knew that she was my baby! Echo's mother was saved from a high-kill shelter, and she was eight weeks old when I got her. Shasta, too, had been scheduled to be euthanized the day we learned about him, and we rushed eight hours each way to Chico, California, to adopt him. He's been an amazing addition to our family ever since.

My husband picked me up at LAX one evening, and we cut through Beverly Hills to avoid freeway traffic. As we were going down Sunset Boulevard, we saw a black dog wandering in the street, and with the dark closing in we worried that a car could speed by and not see him. We stopped and he came to us immediately and snuggled affectionately. I rang doorbells one after another to see if someone was missing him. Nope, and by the time I got back in the car, he was sitting on my husband's lap behind the steering wheel as if he had happily just moved right in and chosen us. The next morning the vet told us that he was microchipped, and when I called the original owners they said that they didn't want him. We were shocked because Graham is the sweetest, most well-behaved dog you could ever imagine, and he shows how grateful he is with us.

I always knew that there was a need to adopt rescue dogs who need good homes. Initially I had no idea how many dogs were euthanized each year in shelters. Once I started volunteering for dog rescues, I was able to grasp the reality of the numbers of how many dogs are killed each year, and I was absolutely shocked. It broke my heart. Part of me wanted to save as many as possible, but part of me knew that I should only take the number of dogs that I knew that I could personally give the full attention that they deserved, and then just volunteer at rescue shelters on top of that.

From childhood till now, my heart had been captured by a love for dogs. Each one of our dogs had pulled on my heartstrings in a very personal way, and I knew that my four absolutely had to be part of our family. Our newest puppy is Marina. She is a blond blue-eyed puppy, half husky and half German shepherd. I had been having dreams about adopting a blue-eyed husky puppy, so when Gabi actually told me about this litter of rescue puppies, I knew Marina was meant to be the new member of our family!

Our dogs have enriched our lives in so many ways, I don't even know where to start. My husband and I have gotten constant love and affection, amazing cuddles, motivation to exercise with the dogs, bonding that happens while training with them, the joy of getting to know and understand and appreciate their individual personalities, and so much more that makes our lives wonderful.

Emma and Arthur

Healing the Brokenhearted

Ellen and Chuck Scarborough

It was destiny that brought Emma into the lives of Chuck Scarborough, a TV anchor of *News 4 New York*, and his wife, Ellen, who are devoted animal advocates and Samaritans. In fact, the Southampton Animal Shelter Foundation (SASF) honored them for "their continuous support and dedication to the organization." *News 4 New York* showcases dogs and cats from SASF that are available for adoption during its live adoption segment, which airs every Thursday.

Chuck and Ellen already had two rescues, a dog, Oliver, and a cat named Stanley. Oliver was known as The Hero Dog after he selflessly stood his ground against a coyote, giving Stanley time to escape. This brave act earned Oliver the Lewyt Humane Scarlett Award for Animal Heroism, given to animals that perform acts of heroism and bravery to save another animal. Ellen said, "The Animal League testified Oliver exemplified the spirit of this award."

Ellen received a notice from Michelle Neufeld Montak of Gimme Shelter about a dog named Sandy and her two pups she had rescued from the Chesterfield County, South Carolina, kill shelter. They were being transported to a New York shelter and needed foster homes while Michelle looked for a forever home.

Ellen didn't stop to think about what she needed to do and rushed to the shelter.

Although the puppies were in extremely bad medical condition, Michelle had found foster homes for them through her network, but Sandy still needed a foster home.

When Ellen saw Sandy, she thought, "This dog has the saddest face I have ever seen on an animal. It was as if all the pains of the world were written on it." Ellen looked into the dog's eyes, and felt the pain this dog had suffered and asked, "How could I not help?"

She brought the dog home. When Chuck saw Sandy, he felt the same way. By the next day, they decided to keep Sandy and named her Emma.

They soon discovered that, even though Emma had experienced the dispassionate harshness of street life, she was sensitive to the pain of others.

"When Oliver was nearing the end of his life, it was a deeply sad time for Chuck and me. We loved him so much. One day, as I sat under a tree holding Oliver in my lap knowing he would soon be gone, I began to cry. Emma came out of the house and saw us. She slowly walked over and began licking the tears from my face to console me. She could sense my heart breaking," Ellen remembered.

Within a few weeks after Oliver passed, Stanley died suddenly. Ellen and Chuck were devastated. Emma lay at their feet to comfort them.

Just days later, destiny stepped in again. Ellen read another notice from Gimme Shelter about a male stray named Miley that had been rescued from one of the worst neighborhoods in New York City. He was being held at the animal control shelter in Brooklyn. He had only forty-eight hours to find a home before he was put down.

Ellen said to Chuck, "Look at his humble stance."

To which Chuck replied, "Call Michelle and tell her we'll foster him."

This gesture, done in honor of the love they had for Oliver and Stanley, became a second chance for Miley.

When Ellen saw Miley, he was in terrible shape. His spirit was broken. He had been horribly abused. He could barely stand and would not eat. He was starving for food and affection, but did not respond to anything. "He just lay there, as if waiting for death to take him," Ellen remembered.

Ellen immediately took the stray, which she renamed Arthur, to the vet. He was in no condition to bring home.

After an extensive examination, the vet told Ellen the dog was more dead than alive and warned her not to be too optimistic. His eyes and ears were infected. He was suffering from kennel cough and intestinal parasites. He was malnourished and was running a fever. His fur was terribly matted and tangled. Ellen also learned that his inability to stand or walk and his perpetual head tilting was caused by a neurological event, perhaps a blow to his head.

Arthur was put into intensive care. Antibiotics were administered to treat the various infections and fever. Another medication treated his neurological condition. The groomer was unable to brush out his fur, so Arthur was shaved, but the groomer left a little tuft on the end of his tail. Having him shaved turned out to be a blessing because the vet was able to discover an out-of-control skin rash that he treated with a medicinal ointment. Arthur was given nutritious food that began to build up his strength and immunity.

A week later, Arthur was finally responding to the treatments.

When Ellen arrived at the vet's office to get Arthur, she couldn't believe the difference. Arthur's dull eyes were now sparkling a little. She could tell from the new fur growing in that Arthur was not brown; his fur was actually black with small tufts of brown. His frame was beginning to fill out. She held out her arms for him "to come."

Arthur, still wobbly, partly from his ordeal and partly because of his previous brain injury, came to her. She put her arms around his neck and told him, "I'm taking you home now."

Ellen meant a permanent home with Emma, Chuck, and her, not a foster home. She didn't know for sure if Arthur understood, but "I could feel him relax into my arms as if all the pain and sadness he had ever experienced left him."

Chuck and Ellen watched Emma greet Arthur with the same sensitivity she had shown her and Chuck many times since they lost their beloved pets. There was never any doubt their pets would get along. In the weeks that followed, he flourished under their care and love.

"These wonderful dogs needed love and a permanent home," Ellen said. "However, they came into our lives when we needed help with our grieving. They filled the emptiness left in our hearts after we lost Oliver and Stanley."

The Miracle Dog

Peter Anthony

It helps, as I tell you my story, for you to know that I am a spiritual life coach and author of several nonfiction books. Even with my intuitive background, I was amazed at the wonderful and unexpected journey that called to me in lifesaving ways.

I was awakened with a jolt in the middle of the night; his floppy ears, sad eyes, and sleek coat were visible to me, and I sensed someone pulling on his blue collar. The dream was calling me, begging me for attention, and I felt helpless lying in the rumpled hotel bed, as I visualized him willfully refusing to enter the kennel door. His eyes begged me as the woman tugged on his blue collar and this image haunted me.

The dream jumped to another scene. It was a long deserted road where I was greeted by an old man. The same floppy ears and sleek coat of this happy yellow Labrador retriever bounded joyfully beside me, and ran up and down the dusty road. Then he jumped up on me looking into my eyes as if to say, "Thank you, thank you." What was I to make of this?

I pulled myself out of bed and walked to the window where I had a royal view of Kensington Palace, the famous London scene. I mused as I thought of the dream. The dog's name begins with a "K." I somehow knew this. Immediately I felt what had to happen without delay when I got home to the United States.

The list was long. I knew that he was waiting somewhere in the southwest region of the United States. Never once did I doubt. The message that I received was so strong. I surveyed my list of every dog kennel, clinic, and veterinary office from Texas to Arkansas, from Louisiana to Oklahoma. I had to find him and answer his calling.

People I called and coworkers said, "Are you crazy?" They snickered, they rolled their eyes, and laughed at my longing to find a dog that I had just dreamed about. The hang ups and ridicule were more reminders that my search was still in vain. But I knew in my gut that all it would take was the right person, circumstance, or chance that could make my incredible and hard-to-believe story come true. With each disappointment, I returned to my quest to find my yellow Lab.

Weeks turned into months, as I persisted, and my dream in London seemed like just that, a dream. "Don't give up," were the kind words of a friend. "If he is out there, you will find him." I hung on to those words as my heart twisted and my spirit bounded. More calls, as I whispered to myself, "Where is my dog that calls me? How do I know what I see and hear is real? God, can you please give me a sign?"

Kelly is on the line for you," my receptionist said, as I bolted past her desk.

"Don't know her," I said, as I kept walking.

My receptionist then replied, "She says that you called her several days ago. She's called you twice this morning." This stopped me in my tracks, and I raced to my phone. The voice on the other end said, "I think that we have your dog." My words did not come easily, as I froze and then stumbled to respond.

"Are you still there?" she asked. She then followed up with, "How did you know about the Lab?"

My voice cracked as I asked, "Does the dog you are boarding come from challenging circumstances, perhaps neglected, and is his vision impaired? Oh, yeah, and his name begins with the letter 'K.' It's just a feeling that I have that I know him," I offered without telling her about the dream.

"All of your descriptions seem to qualify for our kennel to call you," I heard on the phone, "except one. His name is Cody with a 'C' not a 'K,' as you said. His vision is impaired, and his previous owners were neglectful. Our shelter is so crowded now, if he isn't the right dog, we'll unfortunately have to put him down. Can you come right over?"

"Absolutely!" I shouted into the phone.

I had one last question: "Does he wear a blue collar?"

"Yes, how did you know that? You're freaking me out! We'll see you when you get here. Good-bye," Kelly said, and I felt my nerves shoot out of my body in excitement.

"What if? . . ." . . . "Is it really? . . ." My brain spun and I steadied my hand on the steering wheel while racing to the kennel. It seemed like a lifetime. And then, the door opened, and I saw his smooth golden fur. As he broke loose, tail whipping back and forth, he leaped toward me at warp speed and bounded around me in unabashed joy. I saw the blue collar and my heart sang. This is my dog! Cody looked at me as if to say, "Yeah! You found me, good going!"

"This is amazing! Cody has been terribly withdrawn, in pain, and distressed. We've had to force him into his kennel because he willfully refused to enter it. He is so changed," Kelly said. I sat down on the floor and Cody immediately jumped into my lap and licked my face. Call it what you will, but somehow God had a hand in this, I thought, as I was wrapped in the joy of the moment. Dog kisses were too many to count. One could say that a miracle of love found its way all the way from the gates of Kensington to the doors of the rescue shelter.

I learned that even the people at the kennel thought that I was nuts when they had gotten my phone call. However, after witnessing Cody run out the secure door, and down the hall, and then dart over to her desk, Kelly thought Cody might be the dog that was I was inquiring about. They said that if it weren't for Kelly's hunch they wouldn't have called me.

Kelly beamed and leaned in to catch my attention. "Here's Cody's paperwork. You must be psychic!" She chuckled. I winked and said, "What makes you say that?"

"Here's his paperwork from his previous owners. Take a look at the spelling of his name!" Kelly's eyes were wide open with surprise. "His name is spelled with a 'K,' not a 'C'; it was my mistake!" My jaw dropped open, words could not express the rapid sensation of emotion that I was feeling. I wrapped my arms around Kody's neck, buried my head in his fur, and hugged him with tears.

Two more amazing things happened. Kody and I were on our daily gratitude walk one day in the mountains. In the distance of the long dusty road, I saw an old man coming toward us. As we came together, the old man bent down to stroke Kody's head. He looked up at me and said, "Your dog came into your life for a reason, watch over him. Someday he will save your life." I pondered this as he moved away.

Years later, Kody and I were hiking in the San Jacinto Mountains, outside of Palm Springs, California. It was a warm beautiful Easter Sunday morning, with bright blue skies. As we made our way along the trail, Kody spied what I didn't see. Just inches away from my foot was a coiled-up rattlesnake, tongue black as the night. Its diamond-shaped head was perched with one intention: to strike.

Time pauses. The next few moments are chilling. The snake extends its slithery body and lunges toward my knee. Kody steps forward and yanks the snake away. Three clinching bites go to Kody. One bite goes to his face. The second bite goes to his shoulder. The last strike to his leg. The fatal clock has begun. I panic.

"Dear God!!!" Those words echo loudly in my head. My heartbeat pounds inside my throat. Kody is stunned. He falls to the ground. His facial expression shows pain. I pick up a large rock and hurl it at the beast. I reach down and pick up my eighty-five-pound dog and carry him down the mountainside. Sagebrushes cover the landscape. Rocks jut out like fortress walls, perhaps hiding more slithery predators. The weight of my dog strains my descent down the mountain path. Precious moments become a ticking time bomb.

I lay Kody inside the backseat of my SUV. His mouth froths. His panting becomes irregular. I watch my dog slowly succumb to the snake's poison in the backseat of my car. I deparately call the animal clinic.

"Good morning. This is the emergency clinic. May I help you," a voice says.

"Oh, my God, you're open? Um, my dog was bitten by a rattlesnake about an hour ago. Where are you?"

Doors burst open. I cradle my dog into the emergency clinic full of faces I will never forget. A Hispanic family comforts their small children's pain as a tech announces the death of their puppy, a victim of a hit-and-run. An old lady cries with such remorse regarding her cat's death, every person in the room feels her pain. Tears of fear and loss dominate this Easter morning gathering, as a tech rushes Kody into the emergency room. All eyes watch. We wait. We hope. We pray that this Easter morning shows us all mercy.

One by one, every person in the room hears those dreaded words: "We are so sorry." I look at the clock. I look at the emotional devastation that the death of an animal brings to those families that loved them dearly. Then my moment arrives. The tech approaches me. His eyes say it all. Tears roll down my face. My hands tremble. I look down at my feet as though this will soothe my pain.

"Unfortunately, the window of time became critical. Kody won't make it through the night. You are more than welcome to leave him here," he tells me.

Every pet owner's face looks at me. Their tears become my tears. I am stunned. I can't swallow. My body quakes with a hurt I can't begin to describe unless you've walked in shoes of loss.

"No," I say. I will take him home with me. He needs to be home in his bed. Not here in an unfamiliar place." I quiver. I cry. I wipe the tears from my face. I leave the clinic with my best friend doped up on medicine. The ride home is silent.

Depression chisels itself deep in my soul as I enter my condo. Kody's favorite toys line the hallway as I make my way to the bedroom. I lift Kody onto my bed and pet his sweet face. "I am so sorry," I say over and over. His eyes close. His body goes still. His breathing stops. I hold him close to my chest. "Forgive me. Forgive me." I close my eyes and enter a deep sleep.

A ringing phone jolts me out of bed. "Hello?" I answer. "Mr. Anthony. This is Dr. Wendy Beyer from VCA animal clinic. I got your message just now, regarding Kody. We were closed yesterday and . . ."

"Oh, my God," I shout. "Kody is gone. Hold on." I rush down the hallway and hurry to the kitchen. Lapping water from his bowl, Kody is a sight to see. He wags his tail, runs to retrieve his Bullwinkle stuffed animal toy, and proudly escorts it back to me. I pick up the other phone line and yell into the phone.

"He's alive. He's alive!"

R evolving doors open to nonstop ringing phones. Pet owners are abundant. Seats are not. I am greeted by Dr. Beyer with a smile. Her staff looks on Kody and me with amazement. Or is it shock? I suppose it could be both?

"I spoke to the emergency clinic this morning. Kody was not given anything other than Benadryl. No anti-venom. This is remarkable! There is no way a dog could survive three snake bites especially to the leg and shoulder" she tells me.

Everyone looks on Kody with disbelief. Dr. Beyer stares at me with astonishment and says, "This is a miracle dog!" I will never forget those words. Nor will I forget London. Or K-9 Rescue! Or, the old man's smile! And when people ask me if I believe in miracles, I simply say, "Yes." I look whoever in the eye and finish with a simple comment: "I also believe that dreams come true."

"The Person" Named Harry

Charisse Keck

September 14, 2008, is a day I will never forget. I had just lost my first adult pet, roommate, and best friend—Dakota, a chocolate-colored Labrador retriever. In many ways, she was an unplanned rescue. I was young, insatiably curious about Hollywood, and in an emotionally volatile relationship, when Dakota, his dog, fell sick.

It had to have been somewhere around 2 a.m. on a cold foggy night in his Huntington Beach apartment when we both awoke to Dakota throwing up violently on the floor. I had to be in my office in downtown Los Angeles at 8:00 in the morning, and unable to go to sleep, I decided to leave Huntington, beat the traffic, escape his anger at the dog, and head back to Los Angeles.

Somewhere in the process of gathering up my clothes in a sleep-deprived haze, I realized Dakota was sitting in the passenger seat of my BMW. I asked her to leave the car and go back inside so I could race across the 405 Freeway and make it home to my own bed to recover a few hours of sleep before my hectic Monday schedule. Dakota would not get out of the car, and with a pleading in her eyes I will never forget, she begged me to take her home with me.

It took only a heartbeat to decide that on this day we would both make our great escape from that toxic relationship. I put the car in gear and left behind everything negative he represented.

Dakota was my best friend, my salvation, my everything.

Dakota was fourteen when she passed away of heart failure at the vet's office. He assured me that fourteen was a long life for her breed. As soon as I got home, I called my mother, hysterical and overcome with grief, to let her know about Dakota's passing.

Her first words were, "We have to get you a new friend immediately! I'm calling Chrissy at Pet Rescue!"

I don't always agree with Mom, but in this case, she couldn't have been more right. She knew having a dog would help me get through the late-night hours and my chronic fear of the dark. Still in a state of shock, but with reluctant excitement, I grabbed my darkest sunglasses and raced down the 10 Freeway to meet Mom and Christine at the rescue facility.

As I walked into The Pet Rescue Center, I was greeted by a chorus of wailing, imploring dogs, all vying for my attention. Mom was holding a small, blond, and coffee-colored mutt. As soon as she set him onto the floor, he came running to me as if he had found his long-lost best friend. He pawed at my legs as if to say, "Pick me up . . . now!"

As the dog jumped up and down and ran around my legs, Christine explained that Scooter came from an abusive home and ran away three times before a neighbor finally brought him to the rescue center. I could empathize with how he must have felt running through the rural streets of the Coachella Valley in the dark to escape the abuse. I had done it myself years ago. The difference was Scooter was returned to the abusive home two times previously before he finally escaped his worst nightmare. He had only been at Pet Rescue a few hours, arriving about the same time Dakota passed.

I scooped him up, and he wrapped his little legs around my neck. I instinctively cradled him in my arms as I would a baby. I looked down at his deep brown eyes and tiny brown freckles on his nose, and said, "Let's go home, Harry Bond Keck." I chose his name in the tradition of all firstborn males in my family for three generations. They have all been H.B.K., and I wanted Harry to follow in their footsteps.

One of his nicknames is "The Person" because of the humanlike quality in his eyes. We have conversations and somehow Harry knows what I'm saying and feeling. When I'm ill, he snuggles all fourteen pounds of fluff as close as possible to the body part that hurts. When I'm excited, he shares it by running in circles trying to catch his tiny tail.

Harry has traveled with me to New York, Dallas, Miami, Las Vegas, San Francisco, and even Europe. He sports a Louis Vuitton collar and his closet houses a USC jersey he wore when he attended classes with me as I was earning my second master's degree. When my brother graduated from UCLA, he bought Harry a UCLA jersey.

Numerous Los Angeles restaurant chefs know what Harry likes to eat: unseasoned grilled chicken, chopped into little pieces, so he can chew them easily. When we eat at our favorite upscale Los Angeles restaurant, which allows dogs outside on their patio, Harry has five ties from which to choose. In past Halloweens, I have dressed him as a devil, superhero, matador, knight, skeleton, and this year, he will be a fighting ninja.

I always include Harry in my vacations and time off. My friends know that when they invite me to happy hour, a hike, go shopping, get coffee, or eat dinner, Harry will be there, too. Every time I leave the house with Harry, some people ask what breed of dog he is, and I just say he's a "Heinz 57 variety." Others want their picture taken with Harry and proudly pose next to him. Several celebrities, including the former California governor Arnold Schwarzenegger, have petted Harry.

Harry rescued me in many ways. He is the glue that keeps my life on track when I feel down. He has shown me how to appreciate the little things in life that many times I overlooked, such as a clear summer sky in Los Angeles or the warm sand between my toes while taking walks on the beach.

Harry and I enjoyed a weekend away at the Four Seasons, a pet-friendly hotel, in Las Vegas. He swaggered down the hall with more pride than a lucky high roller. I know it was more than destiny that brought Harry into my life. I truly believe Dakota sent him because she knew the love I was capable of giving to my "best friend."

About the Contributors

PETER ANTHONY is a spiritualist life coach, motivational speaker, and author of several nonfiction books. His quick rise to working with the who's who in showbiz began at CBS, where he worked alongside Dan Rather, Diane Sawyer, Lesley Stahl, and Bob Schieffer.

LISA ARTURO is an actress and devout animal rescue Samaritan. She is referred to by many as a rescue angel. She has saved many animals from death's door and is a volunteer at the West Los Angeles shelter, as well as at many other shelters around Los Angeles.

KAYE BALLARD has been on the cover of *Life* magazine, played the Tooth Fairy on *Captain Kangaroo*, and sipped tea in the Bronx with Mother Teresa. Kaye has performed in both burlesque and vaudeville, and before discovering the musical theater, toured with the Spike Jones Orchestra for two years as featured vocalist and tuba player. She appeared on many talk and variety shows, including *The Jack Parr Show, The Tonight Show with Johnny Carson, The Steve Allen Show, The Perry Como Show, The Carol Burnett Show, The Mike Douglas Show,* and *The Muppet Show*. Kaye has had quite a career and today resides with her beautiful rescue dogs in Rancho Mirage, California.

ADRIENNE BARBEAU is an actress and author. Adrienne came to prominence in the 1970s as Broadway's original Rizzo in the musical *Grease*, and as Carol Traynor, the divorced daughter of Maude Findlay (played by Bea Arthur), in the sitcom *Maude*. Adrienne's career has been diverse: she has starred on stage, film, and television; hosted a talk show; authored three books; and done voice-over work. She is still very active and loves it all!

LANCE BASS is an American pop singer, dancer, actor, film and television producer, and author. He grew up in Mississippi and rose to fame as the bass singer for the pop boy band 'N Sync.

LISA BLODGETT has been involved in rescuing and saving dogs for the past fifteen years, and in that time, she has rescued and saved over a hundred dogs. Through her volunteer efforts at the Indio Animal Shelter, and subsequently her involvement in organizations, such as Rescued Hearts Northwest, Alternative Humane Society, Bonerz Advocacy, Rescue Center in Alberta, Canada, combined with her relationship with Wings of Rescue, those dogs have been saved from death row in Southern California shelters, and have found new forever loving homes in the Pacific Northwest and Canada.

LAURA CHAMBERLIN is a reformed New Yorker who loves the desert and has discovered that she loves dogs, too. Now approaching sixty she has decided to start again and open her own business. One of the many benefits that she sees is being able to bring Spencer to work with her. Life is good and Spencer makes it better!

CHEVY CHASE is a comedian, writer, and television and film actor. Born Cornelius Crane Chase, his grandmother gave him the name Chevy when he was two years old and he has gone by that name ever since. Chevy, who was a part of the *Saturday Night Live* crew, embarked on a highly successful movie career. Chevy appeared in the eighties with hits such as *Caddyshack*, the National Lampoon movies, and the Fletch movies. In 2009, he became a regular cast member (Pierce Hawthorne) on the NBC comedy series *Community*. Chevy resides in New York with his beautiful wife, Jayni, and dogs, Chris, Cody, Georgia, and Mabel.

BASIA CHRIST lives in Aliso Viejo, California, after relocating from Chicago, Illinois, in 2001. She has three beautiful children who are the lights of her life, and a wonderful dog, Belle, who is her companion. She is an artist, a writer, and as she loves life!

RENE DELL'ACQUA is a cosmetic dentist in Palm Desert, California. She loves the outdoor lifestyle of the desert and enjoys hiking with her dogs. With four animal shelter rescues, she says, "The relationship with these dogs is like no other. They are the most loving dogs I have ever had. My heart is full, knowing that they are happy now." She is also the mother of three children.

ANDREA GREEVEN DOUZET is the publisher of *Manhattan, Front Desk New York,* and *Beach* magazines, all part of Modern Luxury. Andrea lives in New York City with her husband and two daughters.

ANDREA EASTMAN started her career at Paramount Pictures as head of casting. She was casting director for *The Godfather* and *Love Story.* She became senior vice president at the talent agency International Creative Management. Andrea has represented movie stars, writers, and directors.

From Smothers Brothers to Super Dave to *Curb Your Enthusiasm,* Emmy Award–winning producer, writer, director, and actor **BOB EINSTEIN** has had a career filled with thrills and good fortune . . . but nothing compares to the joy Willie Mays brings!

DAVID EVANS lives in Southern California, with his wife, Carrie, and three dogs. He is a professional gambler, business owner, and runs a dog rehabilitation center from his home, where patients sometimes become permanent residents. David and Carrie love spending time at home with their dogs, Constantine, Rudy, and their newest addition, Buddy Beans!

NATALIE GARCIA grew up in Albuquerque, New Mexico, and now lives in Los Angeles with her three dogs and a wild Mexican kitten. She works for SWEET Travel company as the animal rescue coordinator and is the founder of Mae-Day rescue, which has led her to fostering and finding homes for 150-plus animals, from the Los Angeles area and from the streets of Mexico.

TAMAR GELLER is a dog trainer who developed The Loved Dog™ method of dog training. She is the founder of the first cage-free doggy boarding and day care center in Southern California called The Loved Dog. Preferring the term "life coach" to "dog trainer," and "well-mannered" to "obedient," she provides insight to millions of dog enthusiasts nationwide as the dog expert on the *Today* show. Tamar has also appeared on *The Oprah Winfrey Show*, Animal Planet, CNN's *Larry King Live*, 20/20, Fox News, *Entertainment Tonight*, *Access Hollywood*, E!, *Good Morning Britain*, as well as in the pages of *USA Today*, *The New York Times Magazine*, *Los Angeles Times*, *Newsweek*, *Us Weekly*, *GQ*, *Men's Health*, among others.

CHRIS GENTRY works in business development for Fiserv and **MICHELE GENTRY** is a senior project manager at Hewlett-Packard. Chris and Michele live with their four dogs, Fiona, Ali, Bella, and Lola, in Monarch Beach, California.

TYRA GOLTER has always been an animal lover. From since she was a baby, all of her family dogs have been rescues, and she has continued this tradition bringing many a four-legged mutt, and a pure-breed or two, into her home and into her heart.

PIA GRØNNING was born in a small town in Denmark, and moved to New York City to model after being discovered by Eileen Ford. She spent thirteen years traveling the world modeling, moved to Los Angeles mostly to act, and has been in several features in Europe. Pia did not like the whole casting scene and instead started her own interior design company. She has worked for lots of movie people, but got burned out after fifteen years, and went back to modeling and doing TV commercials.

AMANDA HEARST is the founder and chair of Friends of Finn. She is also market editor at *Marie Claire* magazine and a blogger for the magazine's Web site, where she writes about sustainable fashion and design. Amanda also sits on the Executive Board of Riverkeeper, an environmental organization dedicated to protecting the bodies of water around New York City. She currently resides in Manhattan with her pup, Finnegan.

ORI and **NATASHA HOFMEKLER** are passionate about health and nutrition. They are the founders of Defense Nutrition, which feature products that are designed to nourish, energize, and support the body's metabolic systems for improved health and performance. They live in Los Angeles with their two beautiful children, three dogs, and two cats.

COPPY HOLZMAN is the founder and CEO of Charitybuzz, which is the global auction platform for philanthropists to do good and live well. Top celebrities and corporations use Charitybuzz to offer unique experiences that raise tens of millions of dollars annually for over two thousand nonprofits around the world. Prior to Charitybuzz, Coppy was one of the founders of Webvan, which was an innovative online grocery delivery business and one of the largest Internet IPOs in Silicon Valley. He spent over twenty years in other high-level senior management positions for Macy's and Federated Department Stores. As a father of three grown socially conscious adults, he is now thrilled that he can bring Biggie to work with him every day at Charitybuzz.

LOGAN HOLZMAN was born in Westport, Connecticut, and graduated from Tulane University in 2011. Logan works at Charitybuzz to raise money for thousands of different charities. Her particular interest is in charities that support animal rescue efforts, such as Used Dogs in New Orleans. Logan lives in Williamsburg, Brooklyn, and you can catch her walking around with her pup, Houston.

SARAH JANG has been trained in fine arts and has worked in the arts, media, and publishing industries. She is also a certified yoga instructor, and lives with her husband and Abby in Southern California.

SHIRLEY JONES is an American singer and actress of stage, film, and television. In her six decades of show business, she has starred in a number of well-known musical films, such as *Oklahoma!*, *Carousel*, and *The Music Man*, and won the Academy Award for Best Supporting Actress for her role in *Elmer Gantry*.

CHARISSE KECK graduated from the University of Southern California with a master of arts in professional writing and communication management. She teaches creative writing at the university, is represented by the Gersh Agency in Beverly Hills, and is working on her first novel.

LYNN KINCAID raised three children in Hermosa Beach, California, moved to Indio, California, nine years ago with her husband, and built a small ranch. They have four amazing dogs and several horses. She is living her dream!

CHRISTINA KIRK is a sales professional that lives in the Houston, Texas, area. She loves dogs and if money were no object, she would quit her day job and just go to the dog park all day. She has never met an ugly dog, and she prefers dogs over most people.

HODA KOTB is a television news anchor and TV cohost of the fourth hour of *Today* with Kathie Lee Gifford. Hoda won a Daytime Emmy Award in 2010 as part of the *Today* show team. She is also a bestselling author and a correspondent for *Dateline NBC*.

ELLIE LAKS founded The Gentle Barn in 1999. It was a dream of hers since she was seven years old. Animals were always very healing and nurturing to her as she faced the challenges of growing up, finding herself, fitting in, and feeling understood. She majored in special education and psychology, and with her special love of animals and children, The Gentle Barn became the perfect way of putting all of her talents and passions into one.

RUTA LEE's career in show business began at the famed Grauman's Chinese Theatre. Lee has headlined around the country in many musicals as Dolly, Annie, Molly, Peter Pan, Mame, Irene, Nelly, Irma, Rose, *Woman of the Year*, and

Madame in *The Best Little Whorehouse in Texas*. Ruta and her husband, Webb Lowe, have homes in Hollywood, California; Palm Springs, Florida; Fort Worth, Texas; and Las Hadas, Mexico. She also loves all animals, and is the proud mother of four dogs, two cats, and a big white cockatoo named Samy.

JOHN and **MICHELE LISSBERGER** are avid animal lovers. Since marrying twenty-seven years ago, there hasn't been a time when they wouldn't stop and try to help if they saw an animal in distress. John, raised in Maryland, and Michele, a native of California, first met in Santa Rosa, California. They now reside in Coachella Valley and Big Bear Lake, California, with their wonderful girl, Lucky Lady, who hit the lottery and came to the land of milk and honey, but who would settle for a cookie anytime.

CHRISTINE MADRUGA is a rescue warrior who founded The Pet Rescue Center in Coachella, California. She feels so blessed to be able to live her passion every day. Her motto is: "Our work is never done!"

PETER MARSHALL is a television and radio personality, singer, and actor. He was the original host of *The Hollywood Squares*, from 1966 to 1981. He has almost fifty television, movie, and Broadway credits. Peter and his wife, **LAURIE**, are devoted animal advocates and support numerous animal charity organizations.

Since 1986, **M. MICHELE MARTIN** has been working with real estate clients on the Westside of Los Angeles. Michele has garnered many awards of recognition, and has been honored as a top producer throughout her career. She believes in giving back to the community, and is an honored volunteer at Cedars-Sinai Medical Center with her therapy dog, Rémy. She is also involved with the Center Theater Group in Los Angeles.

TRAVIS MAYFIELD is the owner of Next Level Fitness. Next Level Fitness is a complete fitness and wellness center in California, serving Irvine,

Newport Beach, and Costa Mesa. Buddy, Travis's dog, comes to work with him every day, and Buddy has become the mascot of Next Level Fitness.

MICHELLE NEUFELD MONTAK is the founder and executive director of Gimme Shelter Animal Rescue, a nonprofit rescue organization based in New York. Michelle has devoted the past four years of her life to rescuing animals. Her experience includes the rescue and adoption of approximately 1,800 animals to date from high-kill facilities across the country.

With an incredible eye for what makes a woman feel beautiful, **JENNIFER MILLER** began selling jewelry privately in upscale beauty salons over twenty years ago, then expanded by traveling around the country hosting warmly reviewed and increasingly popular trunk shows. Now with boutiques in New York City; and Southampton and East Hampton, New York; and Palm Beach, Florida, Jennifer's eclectic collection of fine and faux jewelry is unique, and her company prides itself in having something for everyone.

LORETTA MOSHER lives in La Quinta, California, with her husband, Scott, and beautiful daughter, Santana. They were blessed to have their beautiful tabby, Sabina, for sixteen years, and when they had to let her go, Mixer found them, and they are forever grateful.

GEORGE PENNACCHIO is the entertainment reporter for ABC7 *Eyewitness News.* He is also host of ABC7's *Evening at the Academy Awards Pre-Show* and *Post-Show.* During his broadcasting career, George has won three Emmy Awards for his work. He and his wife, **ERIN**, support various greyhound charities devoted to saving the dogs once their racing days are over.

CARYN ROSENTHAL, a former Benny Hill Babe, does voice-overs and commercials. She is also the coauthor of *DUMPED: A Guide to Gettin' Off Your Ass and Over Your Ex in Record Time.* She and Jax—her six-pound mutt who thinks he's a two-hundred-pound, four-legged Rottweiler—live in New York City.

CHUCK SCARBOROUGH is an American television journalist and author. Since 1974 Chuck Scarborough has been the lead male news anchor at WNBC-TV, the New York City flagship station of the NBC Television Network. He has also appeared on NBC News. Chuck currently anchors weeknights at 6:00 p.m. and 11:00 p.m. on WNBC. **ELLEN SCARBOROUGH** is an interior designer and antiques dealer. She has a background in art history, foreign study, and an MBA.

Husband and wife, **COREY FIELD** and **HEATHER SCHMIDT**, live in Los Angeles. Heather is a pianist, composer, and filmmaker, and Corey is a copyright and entertainment lawyer.

DAN SHAW is retired and resides in Indian Wells, California, with his husband, Joel. Dan is an avid horse lover who enjoys spending time with his horses, Felix and Pierre, and he is an active member of the Hunter Jumper equestrian community.

LISA SICKLER WATTS is an executive director managing two medical spas in Beverly Hills and Santa Monica, California, for two world-renowned plastic surgeons. Lisa also owns and operates her own supplement company, Molecularbody. In her spare time she volunteers for Meals On Wheels. This extremely active woman still has time to be a mother to her four children, including three very active human boys and their beautiful golden Lab who thinks he is human. The only female in the house, she keeps all her boys healthy and happy.

JAMIE-LYNN SIGLER is an actress and singer. She is best known for her role as Meadow Soprano on the HBO television series *The Sopranos*. Jamie-Lynn resides in Los Angeles with her fiancé, Cutter Dykstra, their beautiful baby, Beau, and adorable pooch, Bean.

DANIELLE TOWNSEND resides in Gilbert, Arizona, with her husband and four children. She works with children who have special needs in the special education system.

BILL VOLPI is president of his New York–based company Urban Source. Urban Source represents many leading home goods manufacturers, some of which include: Rosenthal, Versace, Joseph Joseph, Breville, and PPD, and many other manufacturers. Bill recently opened Cucina & Tavola factory store, which showcases Paderno, Rosenthal, and Sambonet. Cucina & Tavola is located in Williamsburg in Brooklyn, New York.

MICHAEL and **MARCY WARREN** have been married for twenty-five years. They met when Marcy was a sales associate for The Warren Group, a large apparel group started in 1967 by Michael's father, the late David Warren. Michael held the title of vice president until they sold the company in 1996. They reside in New York City and Water Mill, New York, with their son, Andrew. They have three dogs—Goodman, Panda Bear, and Foxy Lady—and an African gray parrot named Larry Bird. As advocates for several animal rescues, something they feel strongly about, they will continue their mission "To Adopt Don't Shop."